A DECORATOR'S GUIDE

THE COOKIE COMPANION

GEORGANNE BELL

FEATURING OVER **100** UPDATED COLOR FORMULAS!

FRONT TABLE BOOKS | AN IMPRINT OF CEDAR FORT, INC. | SPRINGVILLE, UTAH

For anyone who has ever found themselves
in public with icing on their jeans.
And for S, W, E, A, and little P.

• •

ISBN 13: 978-1-4621-1695-9

Published by Front Table Books, an imprint of Cedar Fort, Inc.
2373 W. 700 S., Springville, UT 84663
Distributed by Cedar Fort, Inc., www.cedarfort.com

LIBRARY OF CONGRESS CATALOGING-IN-PUBLICATION DATA

Bell, Georganne, 1981-
The cookie companion / Georganne Bell.
    pages cm
Includes index.
ISBN 978-1-4621-1695-9 (hardback : acid-free paper)
1. Cookies. 2. Icings (Confectionery) I. Title.
TX772.B4655 2015
641.86'54--dc23
                        2015018129

Cover and page design by M. Shaun McMurdie
Cover design © 2015 Cedar Fort, Inc.
Edited by Melissa J. Caldwell

Printed in China

10 9 8 7 6 5 4 3 2

Printed on acid-free paper

"*The Cookie Companion* by Georganne Bell covers all things cookie, in the fun and funky Lila Loa–style that we know and love. From beautiful, imaginative designs to in-depth color charts, this book is sure to become an indispensable part of every cookie decorator's library. Whether you're new to cookies or an experienced decorator, *The Cookie Companion* has everything you need to make beautifully decorated cookies, every single time."

— **Callye Alvarado**
Creator of www.sweetsugarbelle.com

"*The Cookie Companion* is a must-have book in any cookie decorator's library. With the help of step-by-step tutorials, Georganne's whimsical cookies can be easily recreated by bakers of any skill level. In addition to the cookies themselves, the extensive color mixing and color palette guide made my heart go pitter-patter. Georganne's tips, techniques, and inspiration will have you reaching for your icing bag and apron!"

— **Bridget Edwards**
Author of *Decorating Cookies*
and *Decorating Cookies Party*

"*The Cookie Companion* is an amazing resource, full of tips and tricks that will help anyone become a better cookie decorator. With unique and creative cookie designs this book is sure to inspire. The color chart is a resource that can be used to design a perfect color palette for any cookie theme or platter."

— **Lisa Snyder**
Author of *100 Animal Cookies*
and creator of www.thebearfootbaker.com

"*The Cookie Companion* is a must-have book for cookie decorators of all levels! From the plentiful color chart options and creative cookie ideas, to the endless decorating information this is one book that will certainly help take your cookies to a whole new level!"

— **Toni Miller**
Author of *Cupcakery*
and creator of www.makebakecelebrate.com

CONTENTS

LET'S GET STARTED

COOKIES are kind of fantastic. You put them in your mouth, and they make you happy because they taste like scrumptious little bites of love. But did you know that cookies can also LOOK incredible? It's true. And if you wanted to, *you* can learn to make these delicious tasting, incredible-looking cookies in your own home—in your pajamas if you want to. I'm not going to judge you. Cookies are a judging-free zone.

And we are not talking about the stale, crumbling cookie you get from the grocery store that vaguely resembles an octopus but might also be a popular children's cartoon character. We're talking about show-stopping cookies with a depth of texture, vibrant colors, and piping creativity that will keep your eyes moving until you finally give in and take a bite. You know—the kind of cookies you want to take home to show your mother. And your father. And everyone else in your life because you are just so proud that something so delicious and impressive could actually come from your very own kitchen. Let's make those kinds of cookies.

Are you in? Let's get you started. The first thing you need is a good recipe. It's no secret that cookies are meant to be eaten. The recipe should taste like deliciousness in cookie form and should keep its shape when baked. We don't want your tray of bicycles to turn into Halloween amoebas in the oven, do we? I think not. Luckily for you, I've got three fantastic options—Vanilla Sugar Cookies (page 143), Chocolate Sugar Cookies (page 65), and Gingerbread Cookies (page 98). Go check them out and see which ones you already have the ingredients for. I'll meet you back here in three minutes.

Whoa. You were faster than I expected. You know what I love about those recipes? (Besides everything!) They don't have a "chill time" in them. You can just mix up the ingredients and get right to rolling out the cookies. Start with a lightly floured surface. Toss a ball of dough on there and roll it flat. You can use rings that go on the end of rolling pins to make sure everything is the same thickness, or you can put some flat sticks on each side of your dough to do the same thing. Or if you're really brave, you can just throw caution to the wind and eyeball the thickness. I like to roll the cookie dough out until it is about twice the thickness I need, and then carefully lift the dough and rotate it so I'm sure it isn't sticking. Add a sprinkle of flour here and there if anything starts to stick where it shouldn't. You could also roll that dough out between two sheets of parchment paper and save yourself from a floured-up counter.

Once your dough is flat and smooth and the exact thickness you want it to be, grab a cutter, a drinking glass, or even a kitchen knife and start cutting out shapes. Dip the cutters in flour before cutting out each shape. It helps the dough release from the cutter and also keeps the dough from spreading when baked. Bake according to the recipe and allow the cookies to cool completely before decorating.

While your cookies are hanging out on the cooling rack, you can make up some decorating icing to keep your mind off eating them immediately. I prefer Royal Icing with Powdered Egg Whites (page 126) but you can also make Royal Icing with Meringue Powder (page 126) or even try making some Glaze Icing (page 100). You can get more definition with royal icing, but glaze will always have a softer bite. It's really your choice. Try them both and see which one you like better.

Either way, once you've gotten the icing all mixed up, the trickiest part of cookie decorating will be staring you in the face. You need to color your icing and then adjust the consistency. If you ignore everything else I tell you, please listen to me now. Getting the right consistency of icing before you start decorating will be the difference between things ending in tears and ice cream pity parties—and cookies that make you so proud you can't help but throw open your door and show them to the world. (I will not be responsible for startled mailmen.)

The cookie projects in this book use four different consistencies of icing: thin, medium, thick, and extra thick. It's not complicated; it just takes a little time to get them right. Put your icing in a bowl, stir it around, and then pick it up and give it a good tap or two on the counter. If everything settles out into a glossy surface, you've got yourself some thin icing right there. If it takes five to six taps before everything settles out smoothly, that would be medium-consistency icing.

Thick icing doesn't really settle out, even after tapping it on the counter seven or eight times, but it will still move a little on its own if you tilt the bowl. Extra thick icing doesn't go anywhere, even if you turn the bowl upside down. Extra thick icing doesn't like you and will give you the cold shoulder when you try to use it. We will only use extra thick if we have no other choice.

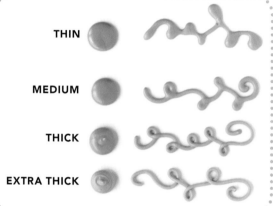

THIN

MEDIUM

THICK

EXTRA THICK

Changing the consistency of the icing is as easy as adding water or powdered sugar. If the icing is too thin, add some powdered sugar. If you have one cup of thin icing, you only need about one tablespoon of powdered sugar to move it up to medium icing. If your icing is too thick, add some water to thin it out. If you have one cup of medium-consistency icing, three to five drops of water should take it down to thin icing. It's not an exact science, so sometimes you will have to add a little powdered sugar, and then a little water, and then maybe some more powdered sugar before you have the icing right where you want it. Trust me though; it will always be worth the effort to get it right.

Icing Cookies

Fit a pastry bag with a coupler and tip. Put the tip down into a small glass and fold the edges over the rim of the glass. Gently pour or spoon the icing into the pastry bag until it is about half full. Overfilling the bags will result in icing smooshing out the top and making a mess all over your precious creations. Don't do that; you won't be happy. You can twist the piping bag or put a clip on the bag above the icing to keep it all inside while you pipe.

1

To fill a cookie with icing, start by touching the tip to the cookie. While squeezing the icing, gently lift the tip just slightly above the cookie so the string of icing touches down on its own. This will keep your outline from getting all squiggly on you.

2

Outline the entire cookie, being careful to touch the icing tip down at any point in the outline where the icing changes direction. Touch the tip down again when you come back to the beginning. You can use either thick or medium icing to outline your cookie.

3

Fill in the middle section with medium or thin icing. The process for filling, or "flooding," the cookie is pretty much the opposite of outlining.

4

You want to keep your tip low, almost touching the cookie. Squeeze the pastry bag so the icing pillows out around the tip.

5

Use the tip to push the icing into corners or smaller spaces. Some people start on one side and go back and forth, while others start around the edges and move toward the center. You can do pretty much whatever you want—start on one side, then go to the other, draw a smiley face in the middle first . . . it all works out the same.

To add dimension, allow one color or patch of icing to dry before adding another. Let the entire cookie dry overnight, or for at least 6–8 hours before attempting to package or stack the cookies.

For more in-depth information on cookie decorating basics, read these entries in the back of the book:

COLORS

COLOR makes our world wonderful. It changes a depressing idea of ever-decreasing light into a stunning and inspirational sunset. It can sway your emotions or communicate danger or excitement. It can also make the most amazing cookies even more incredible . . . or be the bane of your cookie decorating existence if you just can't figure out how to get that perfect shade of green for the moss in your fairy garden cookies. (I would go with Green 14 though, if it were me.)

Can I tell you a secret? I kind of love the adventure of mixing colors. See, food colors aren't actually the pure colors they lead you to believe that they are. Red isn't just red. It has tiny little color ninjas inside, waiting to jump out and surprise you when you mix it with other colors. For example, red and blue food coloring almost never make purple. Usually, they create some shade of brown that might also be pink or green if you look at it in the right light. But yellow and blue DO make green . . . sometimes.

So how do you know what colors to mix together? You have to get to know those ninjas by experimenting. Start with a base color. Take a little icing out of your bowl and mix it with a smidgeon of another food coloring and see where that takes you. You do not want to allow those ninjas into your entire bowl of icing until you're sure you know what they are going to do. Don't be afraid to try a few different color combinations out. You might discover a fantastic new shade of icing that is really and truly fuchsia. A little word of advice though . . . stop when you reach the color of dying foliage. You've gone too far.

I'm not going to lie to you, figuring out how to get the exact color you are looking for can be one of the trickiest aspects of decorating a cookie. It's definitely not impossible, but it can sometimes take more time than you've allotted. Especially since you've already procrastinated getting started in the first place and have exactly 12 minutes to get that icing colored and in the piping bags. What? You don't do that? Psshh. How are we even friends?

Don't give up before you've really begun though, because I have a solution for you! In the following pages, you will find charts with ratios for over 100 different colors. I used Americolor gel coloring because they are widely available, and also because you can squeeze little drops out of the bottle without needing to dig around with a knife or a toothpick. I like that. I used to accidentally put my food color toothpicks on the counter and stain them for life. I did NOT like that.

Before you start flipping around the charts, finding all your dream colors, let's talk about a few things:

- The ideal time to color your icing is after it is mixed, but before you check the consistency. Deep colors can really change how thick or thin your icing is because they use a lot of food coloring. And since we want our consistency to be perfect, color your icing first.

- Portion out the icing you want for a specific color in a small bowl. Add a few drops of food coloring and stir gently with a knife, spatula, or spoon. (I use a knife because I also check and alter consistency with a knife.) Some colors will require a lot more food coloring than other colors. It's okay to keep adding food coloring as long as you are stirring gently and not getting all crazy stirring a bunch of air into your icing like an icing-coloring maniac.

- If you are planning to use multiple colors in one set of cookies, it can be helpful to stir a few drops of each color of icing into the other colors after they are mixed. This will give them a similar base tone and help them look like they belong together.

··

The ratios on the following pages are guidelines. If a color calls for 1 part teal and 4 parts gold, you would start by adding 1 drop of teal food coloring and 4 drops of gold food coloring. To get a darker shade of the same color, keep adding food coloring in the same proportions. For your convenience, 3 different shades of each color—from lightest to darkest—are pictured with every ratio.

It is nearly impossible to get the same size drop of food coloring out of the bottle every single time. Some colors (like brown) are incredibly thin and other colors (like electric pink) are incredibly thick so drops of those colors will be much smaller or larger than the majority of colors. Just do your best to get somewhere in the realm of the same proportions that are listed and you'll be happy. And remember—the icing color, like your cookies, is your creation.

PÂTE DE
GELÉE DOUCE

(Certified Colors (Red 40,
Starch, Vegetable Gum,
(preservatives)
(e of Tartel, fecule de maïs
de sodium, et sorbate de
NET WT. .75 OZ. (21 g)

6 80218 00130 5

Color Charts

Purples

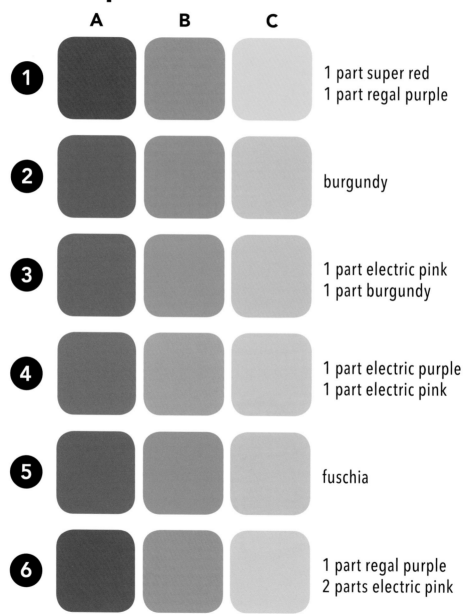

	A	B	C	
1				1 part super red 1 part regal purple
2				burgundy
3				1 part electric pink 1 part burgundy
4				1 part electric purple 1 part electric pink
5				fuschia
6				1 part regal purple 2 parts electric pink

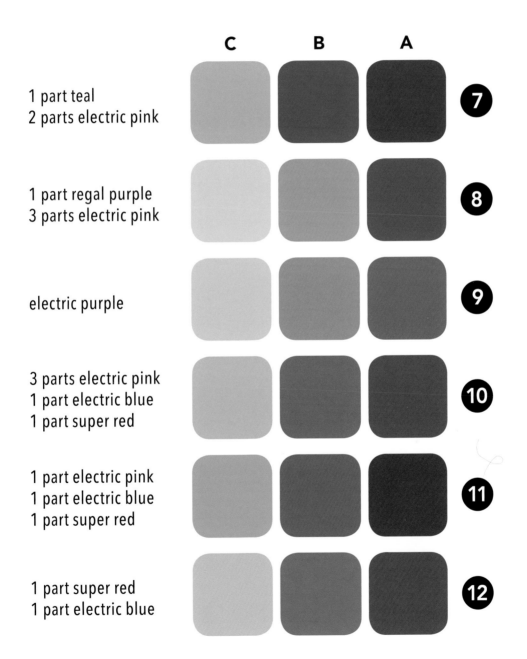

	C	**B**	**A**	
1 part teal 2 parts electric pink				**7**
1 part regal purple 3 parts electric pink				**8**
electric purple				**9**
3 parts electric pink 1 part electric blue 1 part super red				**10**
1 part electric pink 1 part electric blue 1 part super red				**11**
1 part super red 1 part electric blue				**12**

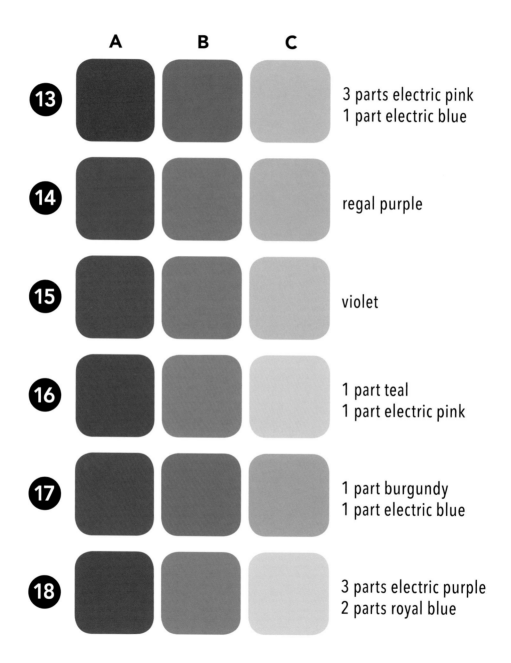

	A	B	C	
13				3 parts electric pink 1 part electric blue
14				regal purple
15				violet
16				1 part teal 1 part electric pink
17				1 part burgundy 1 part electric blue
18				3 parts electric purple 2 parts royal blue

Blues

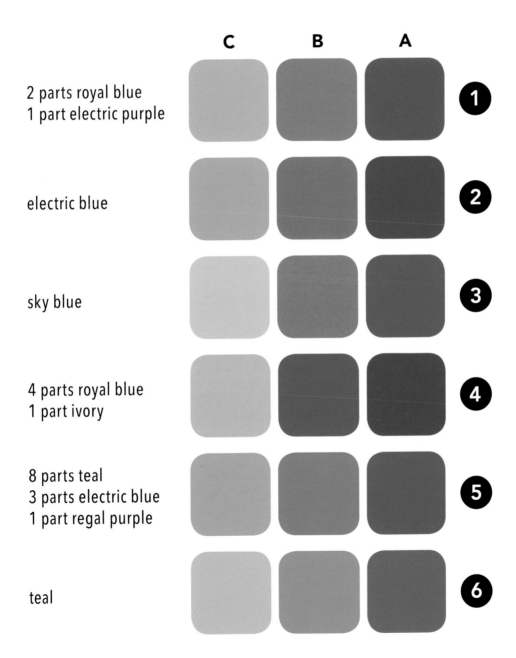

	C	B	A	
2 parts royal blue 1 part electric purple				**1**
electric blue				**2**
sky blue				**3**
4 parts royal blue 1 part ivory				**4**
8 parts teal 3 parts electric blue 1 part regal purple				**5**
teal				**6**

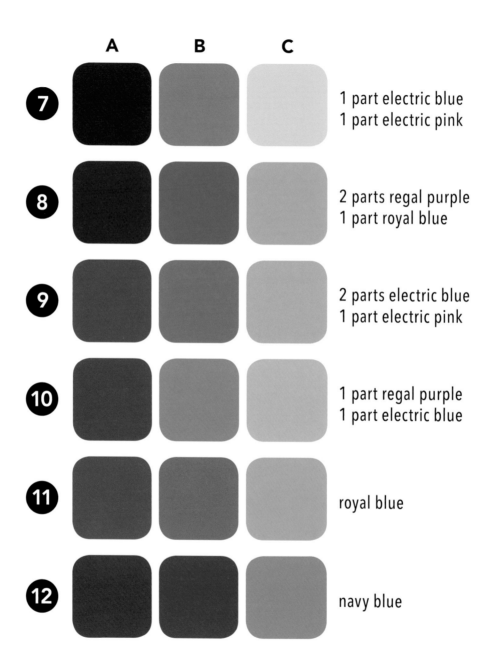

	A	B	C	
7				1 part electric blue 1 part electric pink
8				2 parts regal purple 1 part royal blue
9				2 parts electric blue 1 part electric pink
10				1 part regal purple 1 part electric blue
11				royal blue
12				navy blue

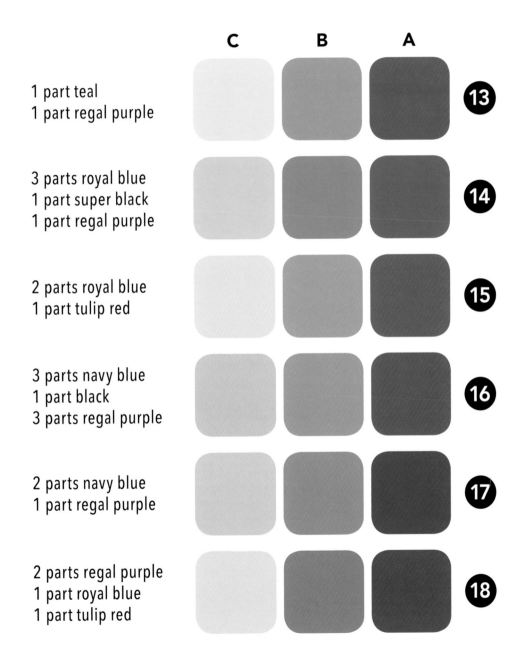

	C	B	A	
1 part teal 1 part regal purple				13
3 parts royal blue 1 part super black 1 part regal purple				14
2 parts royal blue 1 part tulip red				15
3 parts navy blue 1 part black 3 parts regal purple				16
2 parts navy blue 1 part regal purple				17
2 parts regal purple 1 part royal blue 1 part tulip red				18

Greens

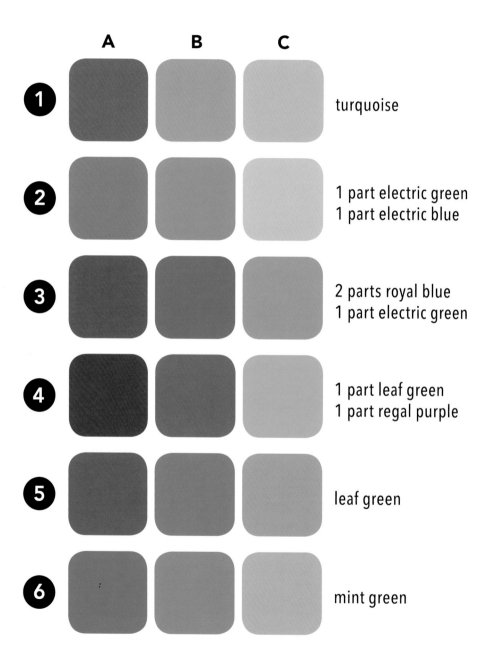

A   B   C

1   turquoise

2   1 part electric green
1 part electric blue

3   2 parts royal blue
1 part electric green

4   1 part leaf green
1 part regal purple

5   leaf green

6   mint green

C **B** **A**

1 part forest green
1 part regal purple
7

forest green
8

1 part leaf green
1 part electric purple
9

2 parts gold
1 part forest green
10

5 parts leaf green
3 parts lemon yellow
1 part chocolate brown
11

3 parts gold
1 part leaf green
12

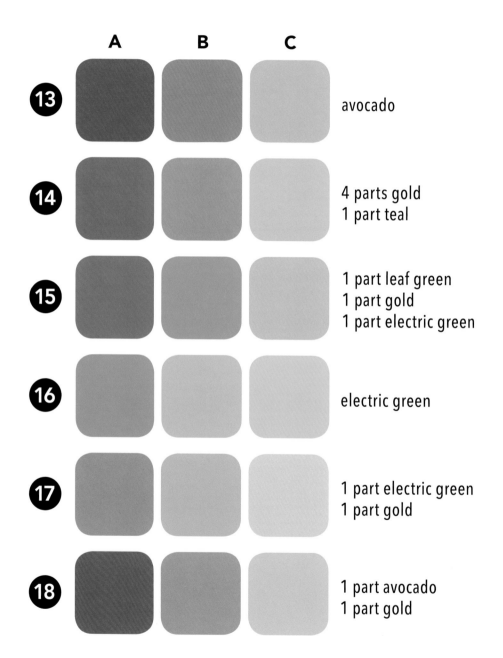

A   **B**   **C**

13   avocado

14   4 parts gold
1 part teal

15   1 part leaf green
1 part gold
1 part electric green

16   electric green

17   1 part electric green
1 part gold

18   1 part avocado
1 part gold

Yellows

	C	B	A	
4 parts lemon yellow 1 part electric green				**1**
electric yellow				**2**
lemon yellow				**3**
4 parts lemon yellow 1 part copper				**4**
egg yellow				**5**
1 part lemon yellow 1 part ivory				**6**

Oranges

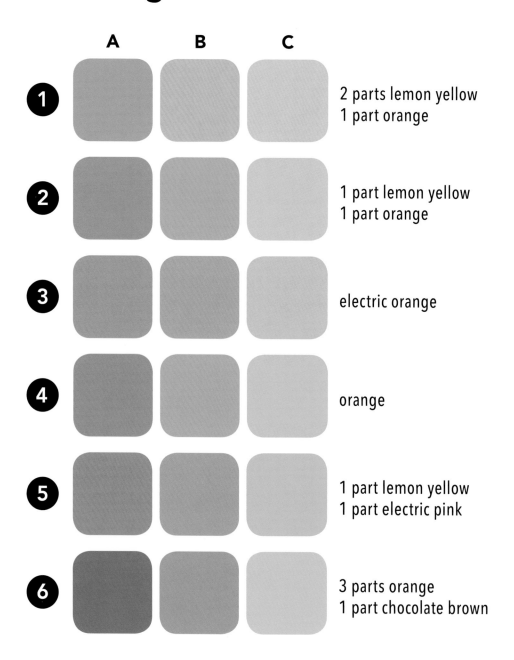

	A	B	C	
1				2 parts lemon yellow 1 part orange
2				1 part lemon yellow 1 part orange
3				electric orange
4				orange
5				1 part lemon yellow 1 part electric pink
6				3 parts orange 1 part chocolate brown

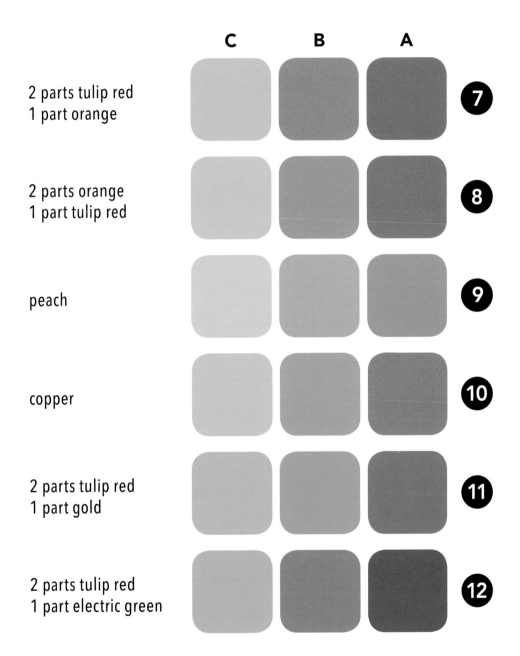

	C	B	A	
2 parts tulip red 1 part orange				7
2 parts orange 1 part tulip red				8
peach				9
copper				10
2 parts tulip red 1 part gold				11
2 parts tulip red 1 part electric green				12

Pinks

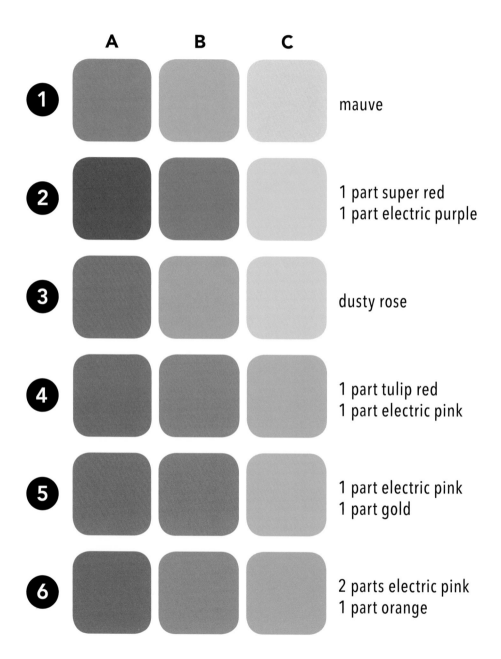

	A	B	C	
1				mauve
2				1 part super red 1 part electric purple
3				dusty rose
4				1 part tulip red 1 part electric pink
5				1 part electric pink 1 part gold
6				2 parts electric pink 1 part orange

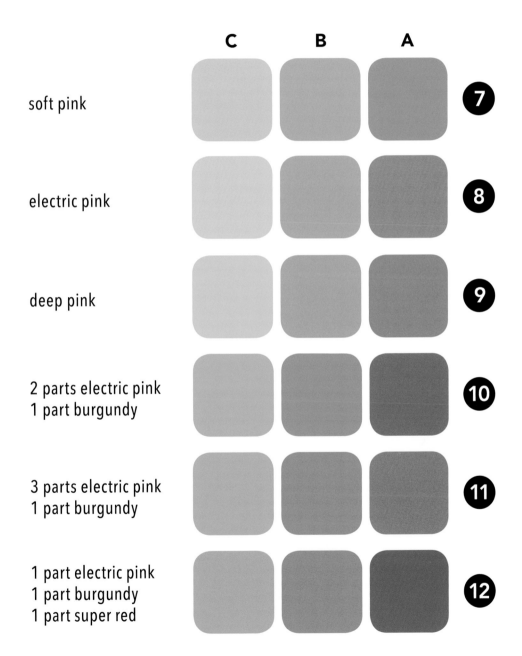

soft pink

electric pink

deep pink

2 parts electric pink
1 part burgundy

3 parts electric pink
1 part burgundy

1 part electric pink
1 part burgundy
1 part super red

C B A

7

8

9

10

11

12

Reds

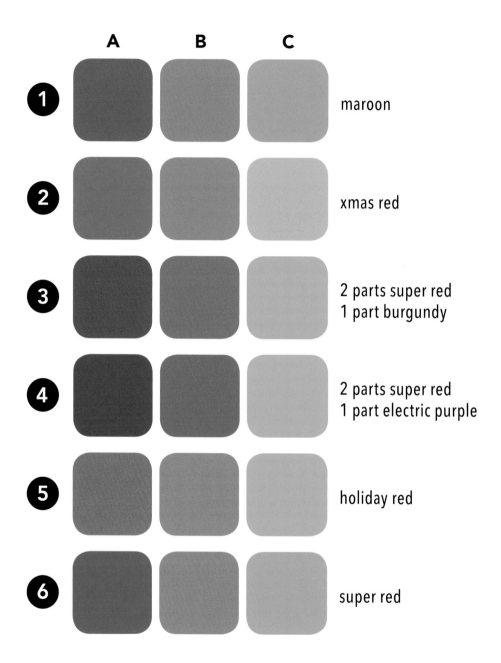

	A	B	C	
1				maroon
2				xmas red
3				2 parts super red 1 part burgundy
4				2 parts super red 1 part electric purple
5				holiday red
6				super red

C **B** **A**

red red — 7

1 part super red
1 part gold — 8

tulip red — 9

terracotta — 10

1 part super red
2 parts gold — 11

2 parts electric pink
1 part electric green — 12

Browns and Black

	A	B	C	
1				4 parts tulip red 1 part chocolate brown
2				2 parts tulip red 1 part chocolate brown
3				2 parts orange 1 part electric green
4				gold
5				ivory
6				1 part chocolate brown 1 part electric green 1 part gold

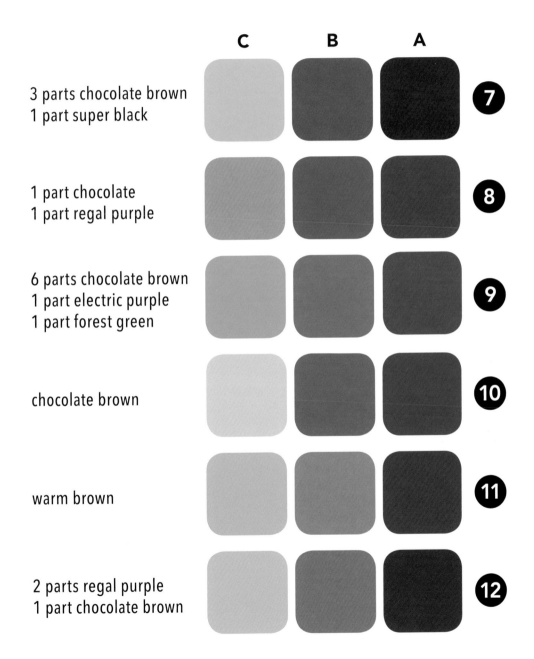

C B A

3 parts chocolate brown
1 part super black — 7

1 part chocolate
1 part regal purple — 8

6 parts chocolate brown
1 part electric purple
1 part forest green — 9

chocolate brown — 10

warm brown — 11

2 parts regal purple
1 part chocolate brown — 12

A　　**B**　　**C**

13 1 part regal purple
1 part gold

14 1 part forest green
1 part chocolate brown

15 1 part chocolate brown
1 part super black

16 2 parts electric green
1 part chocolate brown
1 part super black

17 5 parts gold
1 part regal purple
1 part chocolate brown

18 super black

Color Palettes

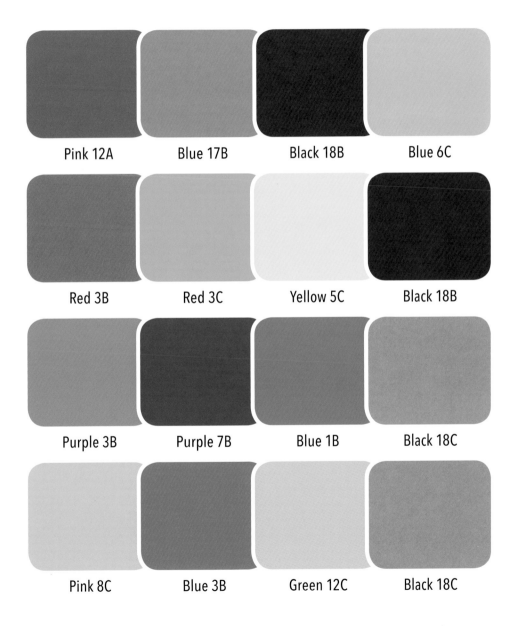

Pink 12A	Blue 17B	Black 18B	Blue 6C
Red 3B	Red 3C	Yellow 5C	Black 18B
Purple 3B	Purple 7B	Blue 1B	Black 18C
Pink 8C	Blue 3B	Green 12C	Black 18C

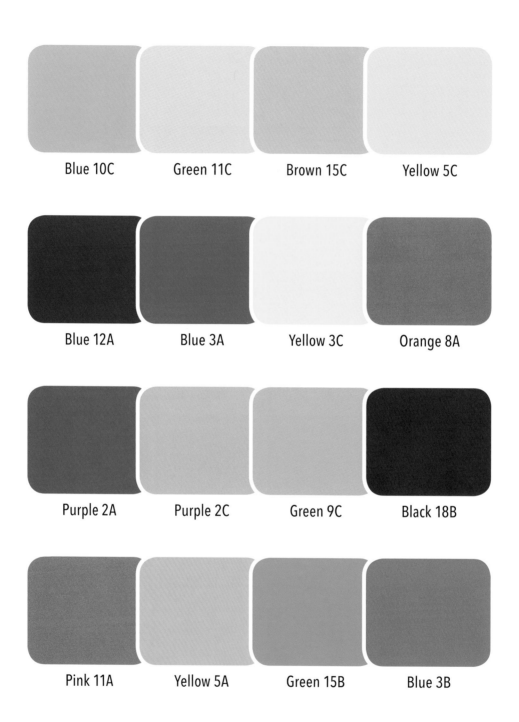

Blue 10C Green 11C Brown 15C Yellow 5C

Blue 12A Blue 3A Yellow 3C Orange 8A

Purple 2A Purple 2C Green 9C Black 18B

Pink 11A Yellow 5A Green 15B Blue 3B

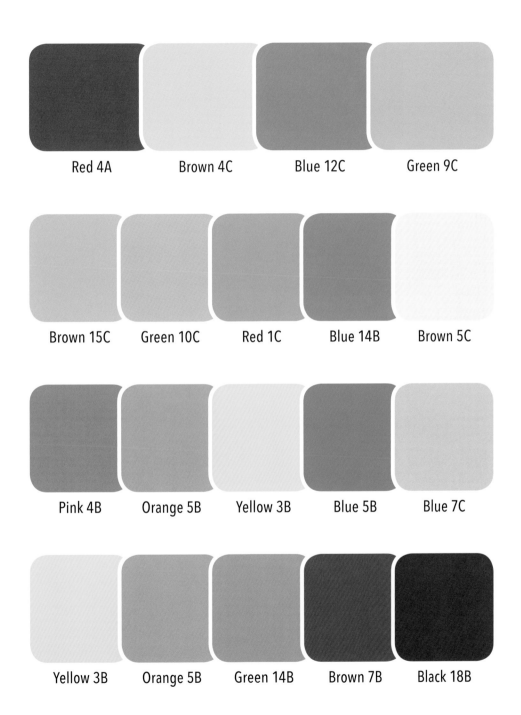

Red 4A   Brown 4C   Blue 12C   Green 9C

Brown 15C   Green 10C   Red 1C   Blue 14B   Brown 5C

Pink 4B   Orange 5B   Yellow 3B   Blue 5B   Blue 7C

Yellow 3B   Orange 5B   Green 14B   Brown 7B   Black 18B

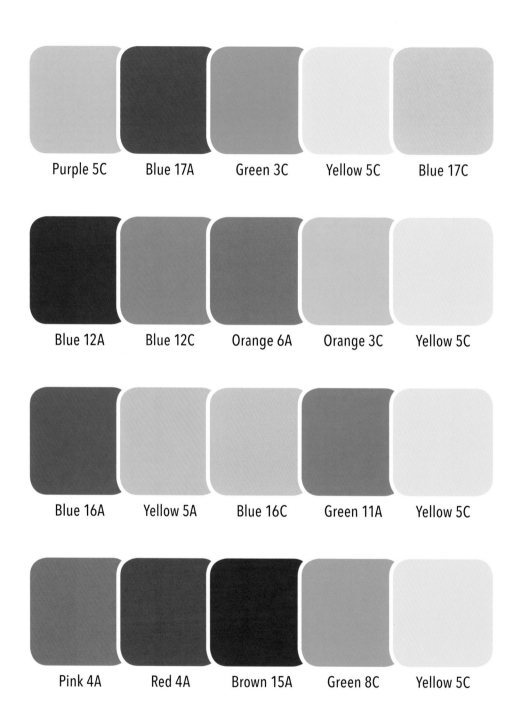

Purple 5C	Blue 17A	Green 3C	Yellow 5C	Blue 17C
Blue 12A	Blue 12C	Orange 6A	Orange 3C	Yellow 5C
Blue 16A	Yellow 5A	Blue 16C	Green 11A	Yellow 5C
Pink 4A	Red 4A	Brown 15A	Green 8C	Yellow 5C

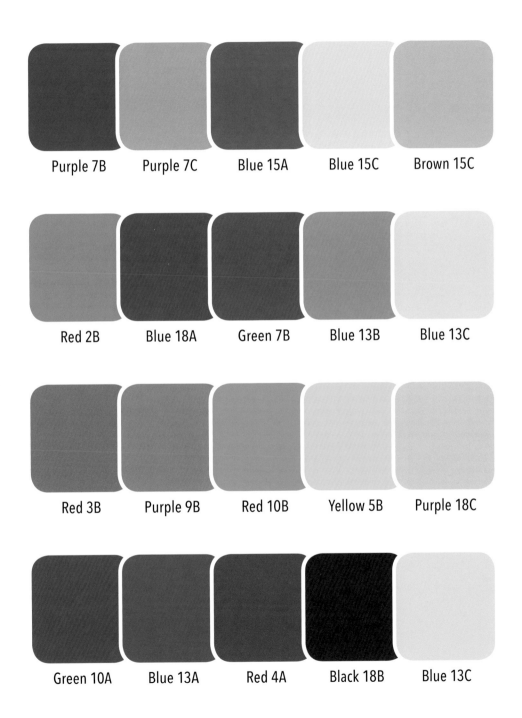

Purple 7B Purple 7C Blue 15A Blue 15C Brown 15C

Red 2B Blue 18A Green 7B Blue 13B Blue 13C

Red 3B Purple 9B Red 10B Yellow 5B Purple 18C

Green 10A Blue 13A Red 4A Black 18B Blue 13C

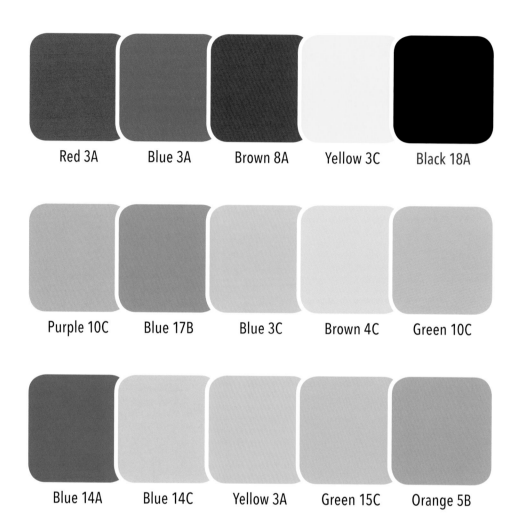

Red 3A Blue 3A Brown 8A Yellow 3C Black 18A

Purple 10C Blue 17B Blue 3C Brown 4C Green 10C

Blue 14A Blue 14C Yellow 3A Green 15C Orange 5B

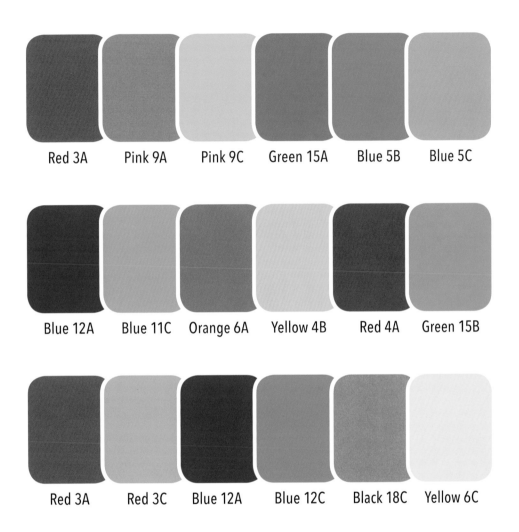

Red 3A	Pink 9A	Pink 9C	Green 15A	Blue 5B	Blue 5C
Blue 12A	Blue 11C	Orange 6A	Yellow 4B	Red 4A	Green 15B
Red 3A	Red 3C	Blue 12A	Blue 12C	Black 18C	Yellow 6C

COMPENDIUM

Airbrush (See also *Stencils*)

An airbrush is a small machine comprised of a compressor, an air hose, and an airbrush gun. Special airbrush food coloring (do not use regular food color) is placed in the cup. When the compressor is turned on and the trigger pulled back, you are able to spray food coloring wherever your heart desires . . . but preferably onto a cookie. It's a great way to add dimension to your cookie project. Airbrushes can also be used with stencils for a quick design or to add interest to a background.

. . . .

Angel

 Use a wide Christmas tree cutter to cut out cookies, and then bake them according to recipe directions.

2 Turn the Christmas tree cookie upside down. With medium skin-colored icing, pipe a rounded heart shape near what is now the top of the cookie.

3 Add flowing white wings with medium-consistency white icing and a #3 tip. Try not to let the wings touch the face. It's okay if you do though. If there is any color bleed, it will be covered up later.

4 Use the same icing to pipe a dress. Leave room at the top to give your angel a neck. Let it dry for 20 minutes.

5 Add arms with the same white icing. Let the entire cookie dry for 4 hours or overnight if you live in a humid environment.

6 With medium-consistency brown icing and a #3 tip, let's give this girl some hair. If you want her to have a part line, pipe one side of the hair first and then wait 5 minutes before piping the other side of her hair. Add a drop of skin-colored icing between her face and the dress for her neck.

7 Use thick yellow icing and a #3 tip to pipe a halo above her head. Pipe a small circle of skin-colored icing at the bottom of each sleeve for her hands.

8 Add some powdered sugar to your white icing to make it a thick consistency. Use a #2 tip to pipe swirly details on the dress. Add eyes with medium-consistency black icing and a #1.5 tip. Alternatively, you could also draw them on with a black food color marker. Use pink food coloring or luster dust and a food grade paintbrush to give our angel her rosy cheeks.

9 Thicken up your brown icing with some powdered sugar and use a #1.5 tip to add details to the hair.

Animals (See *Dog, Fox, Giraffe, Monkey,* and *Zebra*)

B

Baby (See *Baby with Pacifier, Bunny, Pacifier,* and *Ring Toy*)

Baby with Pacifier

1 Use the ice cream sundae cookie cutter and cut out as many cookies as you need. Then use a circle cutter to cut the bottom off before baking.

2 This step is optional. Outline and fill in the entire cookie with white icing. Allow to dry completely

3 With medium-consistency skin-colored icing and a #3 tip, pipe a circle shape near the top of the cookie. Allow to dry for at least 30 minutes. Let it dry longer if the jammies you plan to put on your baby will be dark colored.

4 With medium-thickness blue icing and a #3 tip, pipe on some jammies. I think it's easiest to start with the arms. Then do both sides and then the legs. If I try to do it all at once, things get wonky.

5 Make two little eyes using thick black icing and a #1.5 tip. Use medium-consistency skin-colored icing and a #1.5 tip to make an adorable little nose and two hands. Add a pacifier with thick green icing and a #1.5 tip. Do this by piping a little heart and then round the bottom with a toothpick.

6 With thick blue icing and a #1.5 tip, add a zipper to the jammies and detail outlines on the feet. Use thick brown icing and a #1 tip to add a ring to the pacifier and some hair on that little child of yours. Add eyebrows with the same icing or with a black food color marker. Paint some rosy little cheeks with pink luster dust or with pink food coloring.

Baking Sheets

You can bake your cookies on pretty much anything that is flat. What if all you have is a piece of bark you peeled off a tree and an open fire? You can probably still bake cookies on that. But if you want reliable results every time, may I make a suggestion? The baking pan I use most often is a half-sheet 18-gauge aluminum baking sheet with reinforced edges. A half-sheet pan is roughly 18 inches by 13 inches. It will fit in most traditional ovens while still leaving 3–4 inches around each side for adequate airflow. The reinforced edges help keep the pan from warping when the aluminum gets hot and turning it into a culinary gong. If you can find a baking sheet with encapsulated steel rims, that's even better. Dark pans will absorb heat instead of reflecting it and the cookies will bake faster and hotter. That means you will end up with cookies that are brown on the bottom before the rest of the cookie is fully baked. If you really like crispy cookies, though, dark baking sheets will be your new best friend.

Balloon

1 Use a balloon cutter to cut out cookies, and then bake them according to recipe.

2 Outline and fill the rounded part of the balloon with medium-thickness white icing. Let it dry for 15 minutes.

3 Add the knot at the bottom with the same icing. Let the entire cookie dry for 6 hours or overnight.

4 Place a polka dot stencil over your cookie. Scrunch up a paper towel and grab some medium-consistency red icing with it.

5 While holding the stencil in place, dab the red icing on to the cookie.

6 If you are going for the vintage look, don't worry about filling in all the holes. If you want a cleaner look, try using a scraper with the stencil instead. See **Stencils with Icing** for help with this method.

7 Use the **Vintage** painting technique to age the cookie.

Basket Weave

1 Bake a desired cookie shape. Use a #3 tip and thick icing (any color) to make an odd number of vertical lines in the space where you want the basket weave pattern.

2 Change the tip to a #5 tip and pipe horizontal lines over the top of every other vertical line.

3 The next row should be opposite of the first row. Start by piping a small dot in the spot between the first two vertical lines. Then pipe over the top of alternating vertical lines. Keep your second row of basket weave close to the first row.

4 Continue alternating rows until you reach the bottom of your vertical lines.

5 In case you are wondering, I like to finish the baskets with a line of U shaped scrolls along the bottom and top of the basket.

Beach (See *Mermaid*, *Palm Tree*, *Sand Castle*, *Sea Horse*, and *Starfish*)

Birthday (See *Balloon, Candle, Cupcake,* and *Gift*)

Black Icing (See also *Saturated Colors*)

A true black icing, like other saturated colors, is notoriously difficult to achieve. There are a couple of ways to make it easy on yourself. You can start by mixing all your leftover icing together to create a bowl of icing roughly the color of a swamp and then add a little black food coloring until it reaches a dark gray shade. Or you can add about 1 teaspoon of sifted cocoa powder per 1 cup of brand-new white icing and mix until your icing is roughly the color of a swamp. Then add a little black food coloring until it reaches a dark-gray shade. It will continue to darken over the next few hours.

Blotching

If there was a curse of the decorating world, it would be "The Dreaded Blotch." It seems to happen at random and without any notice. The icing discolors in one or more locations as it dries and the discoloration seems to spread over time. There is nothing wrong with the cookie, but it can be disheartening to decorators. If you find the blotch appearing on your cookies more than you would like, you can brush the tops of the baked cookies with a simple syrup (equal parts water and sugar, boiled until the sugar dissolves) and allow it to dry before decorating.

Brush Embroidery

1 Outline and fill your cookie with the icing color of your choice. Let the base layer of icing dry for at least 3 hours, preferably overnight.

2 Use a #3 tip and thick icing in a contrasting color to pipe a curved scalloped line where you want your first petal to be.

3 You can use any food grade paintbrush you like, but I prefer the angled square brush. Dip it in water and blot the excess on a towel. Holding it vertically, begin to "cut" into the icing, and drag it toward where the center of the flower will be. Continue cutting and pulling the icing along the entire line you just piped. If your icing is too thick or your brush is too dry, the icing will crumble instead of pulling. If your icing is too thin or your brush is too wet, you won't be able to see distinct lines.

4 Repeat steps 2 and 3 to add another petal. Don't try to pipe more than one petal at a time. The right consistency is imperative and if the line sits too long before you start cutting and pulling, the icing will crumble and break instead of turning into beautiful magic petals.

5 I like to add a dot of icing in the middle and sprinkle nonpareils on top for the center of the flower. You can also add leaves in the same color or different colors.

Bubbles in Baked Cookies

If you use flour to roll out your cookie dough, flour and air can sometimes gather between layers of the dough as it gets worked in after each round of rolling and cutting. This will create bubbles in the cookies when they bake. When this happens, you can use the back of your spatula to gently smooth and flatten the cookie surface. If you don't get to the bubbles before they cool, you can always decorate the back of the cookie instead!

Bubbles in Icing

Air is incorporated into the icing while it is being mixed. This creates bubbles that will rise to the surface when the icing is piped onto a cookie. You should probably accept the fact that bubbles can happen to you. It's pretty much inevitable that they will appear, but you can reduce the frequency when bubbles occur. First, when you mix your royal icing, add enough powdered sugar to keep it on the thick side. Second, when thinning your icing and mixing colors, do it by hand and mix carefully so you aren't adding more air to the icing. Third, bubbles will be larger and more frequent in thin icing. Avoid using really thin icing.

Bunny

1 Combine a rattle cutout with the legs from a teddy bear or gingerbread man to create the ears of a bunny. Cut off the knobby bumps at the bottom of the rattle. For more help, see **Combining Cutters**. Bake according to recipe instructions.

2 Use a #3 tip and medium-thickness taupe icing to outline and fill a circle for the head. (Seriously . . . did you know that kind of color was called taupe? I never really knew what taupe was until this moment. Cookies can be educational.) Let it dry for 5–10 minutes or until the surface icing sets.

3 To add the ears, start by piping a circle at the top of the ear. Use the tip of your piping bag to drag the icing toward the head. After piping both taupe ears, immediately repeat this step with pink icing on top of the taupe icing.

4 Outline the shirt area with thick pink icing and a #3 tip. Use thick dark-taupe icing and a #1 tip to add a tiny little heart nose.

5 Fill in the shirt area with thin pink icing and a #3 tip. Immediately add white stripes with medium-thickness white icing and a #2 tip.

6 Add some little arms with the taupe icing and a #3 tip. Just like the ears, first pipe a circle of icing for the hands and use the piping bag tip to drag the icing toward the body.

7 Use thick black icing and a #1 tip to pipe two little eyes. Use the same icing or a food color marker for eyebrows and a mouth. You can paint the rosy cheeks with pink luster dust or pink food coloring.

Butter

Butter comes in two flavors—salted and unsalted. Most baking recipes call for unsalted butter for the simple reason that every butter company is the emperor of their own butter worlds and each uses different amounts of salt in their butter. In order to achieve consistent, precise results, baking recipes use unsalted butter and then use an exact amount of salt for the recipe. I have found that for the cookie dough recipes in this book, the flavor change is minimal between the two types of butter. Not surprisingly, the people that usually use unsalted butter typically enjoy the cookies made with unsalted butter best. And the people that usually use salted butter like the cookies made with salted butter best. The salt content doesn't normally affect the way these cookies bake. It just comes down to personal taste.

Cake

1 Combine a cake cutter and a small X cutter to make a cake on a pedestal. Place together on baking sheet and bake as directed by recipe. A small heart cutter could be used instead of the X cutter. See **Combining Cutters** for more help.

2 Make flower transfers with yellow icing and white nonpareils. Pipe a star shape with medium icing and a #2 tip. The icing will flow together to make a flower shape. When the surface has dried, add squiggly details with thick yellow icing and a #1 tip. Drop a few nonpareils on to each flower. Allow to dry for 4–6 hours. See **Royal Icing Transfers** for more help.

3 This cake is full of ruffles. You need extra thick white icing and either a #101 or a #103 tip. Keep the wide end of the tip down toward the cookie and the narrow end pointed up and toward the top of the cookie.

4 Move the tip up and down as you pipe across the cookie.

5 Continue making ruffles across the top tier of the cake. The number of ruffles you will be able to fit will depend on the tip you are using. Let the top tier of ruffles dry for 30 minutes.

6 Use medium gray icing and a #2 tip to pipe a small zigzag border below the top tier. Add a royal icing transfer flower on top of the gray icing.

7 Add another layer of ruffles and then another gray zigzag border.

8 When you have finished the bottom tier of ruffles, use a toothpick to straighten out the bottom edge of the ruffles.

9 Use thick yellow icing and a #3 tip to pipe a straight line across the bottom of the cake and to add two swirls for the pedestal.

Candelabra

1 Use a crown cutter to cut out cookies, and then bake them according to recipe directions.

2 This step is optional. Outline and fill cookie with medium-consistency white icing. Allow to dry overnight or for at least 6 hours.

3 With medium-consistency black icing and a #2 tip, pipe a triangle for the base and half circles for the candleholders.

4 With the same icing, add a beaded stem from the base to the top half circle, one dot at a time. Allow each dot of icing to set for 2–3 minutes before piping the next one.

5 Use medium-consistency purple icing and a #2 tip to pipe candles on top of the candle holders. With thick black icing and a #1.5 tip, pipe an arm on each side of the base.

6 Add candle flames with a #2 tip and medium-consistency yellow icing. I find it easiest to pipe a small dot for the base of the flame and then use the icing tip to drag the flame up and curve it out. Pipe one more arm on each side of the base.

7 Use a silver airbrush paint to add texture to the candelabra and candles.

Candle

1 Use a candle cutter to cut out cookies, and then bake them according to recipe.

2 With medium-consistency white icing and a #3 tip, pipe diagonal stripes across the candle. Try to leave enough space between them for the same width of lines in another color. Don't worry if it's not perfect. It will all work out. Let the white lines dry for 1–2 hours to avoid color bleed before moving on.

3 With medium-consistency red icing and a #3 tip, add red diagonal lines in the spaces between the white lines. Let it dry for 15 minutes.

4 Add some dripping wax with the same red icing at the top of the candle.

5 With medium-consistency orange icing, pipe a flame on top of the candle. I find it easiest to hold my tip close to the cookie and let the icing pillow out around it into a circle. Just drag the tip through the icing toward the top, creating a flame shape.

6 Add a candle wick with thick brown or black icing and a #1.5 tip.

Cat

1 Cut dough with a pumpkin cutter. Use a circle cutter to make an imprint before baking according to recipe directions.

2 With medium-consistency yellow icing and a #3 tip, outline and fill the moon area of the cookie. Allow to dry for 2–3 hours.

3 With medium-consistency white icing and a #3 tip, add fence panels on the side of the cookie. Let them dry for at least 10 minutes.

4 Add a third fence panel with the same white icing.

5 Use medium-consistency black icing and a #2 tip to pipe an upside down "U" shape for the cat's body. Let it dry for 15 minutes.

6 Add a lemon shaped head and a wavy tail with the same black icing. Let the cookie dry for 2–3 hours.

7 Pipe white lemon-shaped eyes on to the head. Immediately add a green dot and then a smaller black dot to finish the eyes.

8 Use white, black, and brown food coloring to paint fence panels. See WOOD GRAIN for more help.

Chalkboard (See also *Black Icing* and *Painting*)

1 Outline and fill a cookie with black icing and a #3 tip. Allow it to dry overnight or for at least 8 hours. I am not kidding about this step. If it's not completely dry, the black food coloring can creep into the white food coloring and make you cry, or at least make a mess of your carefully painted design.

2 Once you are certain your base icing is really and truly dry, pour some white food coloring into the lid of the bottle. Grab a food safe paintbrush and dip it in some water. Without brushing off any of the water, place the paintbrush's tip into the food coloring to get a small amount of white and then brush it haphazardly across the top of your cookie.

3 Immediately grab a paper towel and wipe the white food coloring and water off the cookie for that "just erased" blackboard look. Be careful to leave enough white on the cookie so it will be visible after you've painted your design. If fibers from the paper towel find their way onto your cookie, you can brush them off with a dry paintbrush.

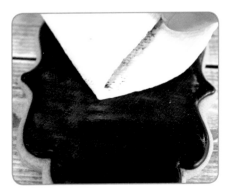

4 Dip the paintbrush back into the water and wipe it carefully on a paper towel so the tip comes to a point. Then dip it very carefully into the middle of the white food coloring. (The food coloring gets kind of gunky near the edges.) I find that smaller brushes are much easier to control. The brush I'm using is a 4/0 spotter brush.

5 With the very tip of the brush, paint whatever you like. Use a very light hand for thinner lines and a heavier hand for thicker, whiter lines. If you've added too much white food coloring to an area, dip your brush in water, dry it on the paper towel, and then use it like an eraser. Any leftover white smudges are just an added bonus!

6 If you want to add color to your chalkboard images, first put down a layer of white food coloring. Let it dry for 20 minutes. Then you can use that fantastic little brush of yours to paint any color you want over the top. Just make sure to brush the color on lightly so it doesn't lift the white coloring up again. If it does, don't give up and spend the night wallowing in ice cream tears. Just let it dry and try again.

Chocolate Sugar Cookies

Are you looking for the recipe for soft sugar cookies that don't spread and taste like brownies? These are the answer to your quest!

Ingredients:

1 cup butter

¼ cup shortening

1½ cups sugar

2 eggs

1 tsp. vanilla

1 tsp. salt

¾ tsp. baking powder

⅔ cup cocoa

3 or 3½ cups flour

Cream butter, shortening, and sugar together. Add eggs and vanilla. Mix well. Add salt and baking powder and mix again. Stir in the cocoa until well blended. Add flour 1 cup at a time.

NOTE: If you are going to make cookies right away, add 3½ cups flour. If you are going to "chill" the dough, or just wait for another day to make your cookies, use only 3 cups. It will be totally soft and look all wrong, and you will want to ignore me completely and add more flour, but I'm telling you—DON'T DO IT. Practice self-restraint. You will be glad you did, and I will be proud of you.

Roll dough out on lightly floured surface. Bake at 375 degrees for 7 minutes if you roll to ¼-inch thick and for 10 minutes if you roll to ⅜-inch thick.

If shortening isn't available where you live, or you just hate it on sheer principle, you can leave it out and add another ¼ cup of butter instead.

Christmas (See *Angel, Christmas Tree, Reindeer, and Toy Soldier*)

Christmas Tree

1 Use a Christmas tree cutter to cut out and bake trees according to recipe directions.

2 Use thick green icing and a #2 tip to outline the sections of the tree.

3 Fill in the lower half of each section with a medium-consistency light-green icing and a #2 tip. Let it dry for 20 minutes.

4 Fill in the top half of each section with a medium-consistency darker green icing and a #2 tip. Carefully pipe over the top of the light-green section to give the appearance of dimension between the boughs on the tree.

5 While the darker green icing is still wet, add sugar pearls or sprinkles for ornaments.

6 Add a tree trunk with medium-consistency brown icing and a #2 tip.

Circles, Baking

If you've ever baked a circle cookie, you've lamented the ease at which cutout circle cookies get wonky. The good news is that there is an easy solution. First, it's super important that you find a recipe you love that doesn't spread. (See **Chocolate Sugar Cookie** or **Vanilla Sugar Cookie** if you need a suggestion.) Begin by cutting out a circle of dough just larger than the circle you actually want. Transfer the cutout in all its wonky, stretching goodness to your baking sheet. Cut the dough again with your smaller, perfect circle cutter. Remove the excess cookie dough and . . . Ta-da! Instant perfect circle for baking. Also, you should know that plastic circle cutters hold their shape much better and longer than aluminum or tin circle cutters.

Circles, Piping

Circles are a simple, recognizable shape . . . and very nearly impossible to re-create perfectly in icing. There are a couple of things you can do to improve your chances of avoiding lopsided circles. If you know where you want your circle, you can use a small circle cutter to make an impression on the cookie before baking. When you lay your line of icing down on the indent, it will roll into the center of the line. If your circle needs to go on top of other icing, you can trace around the small circle cutter with a food color marker to give you a guideline. Whichever method you choose, make sure your icing is at least a medium-consistency. Touch the tip gently to the cookie and pull up as the icing starts to come out. Lay the icing down along your circle guide without touching the tip back to the cookie until you reach the end. Be sure to stop squeezing just a little before you get there so you won't have an excess blob of icing at the start/ending point.

Clumps in Icing

There are a few different things that can lead to clumps in your icing. The meringue powder or powdered egg whites are pretty much born to clump. When you make your icing, make sure you mix them with water and whisk well before adding the powdered sugar. Scrape down the sides of the mixing bowl as necessary to get rid of all the clumps you see. Powdered sugar can be another clump culprit. Sifting your powdered sugar can help. If your powdered sugar is excessively full of lumps, try another brand. They aren't all made equal. Clumps can also happen when the dried icing on the side of a bowl or the surface of the icing is accidentally mixed back in with the rest of the wet icing. There is a solution to all of these causes. Place a piece of fine mesh or nylon over the top of the bag and coupler before placing the tip and ring on the bag or bottle. The mesh or nylon will act as a sieve to keep the clumps and bits of dried icing in the piping bag and not in your tip. If your icing is especially clumpy or thick, it will put more pressure on the mesh/nylon and a double layer is advised.

Color Bleed

When two colors of icing are piped next to each other, the food coloring from one of them can blend itself into the neighboring icing color. This happens most often when saturated colors like red or black are piped next to white icing. Humidity and thin icing both make this worse. To avoid color bleed, allow the first layer or color of icing to dry completely before adding the second layer or color of icing; use the thickest icing you can get away with for your design; and place the cookie near a moving air source, such as a fan, while drying.

Coloring Icing

While it is certainly possible to color an entire batch of royal icing the same color, most of the time you will need to split your icing into smaller bowls and color each of them their own gorgeous shade. Place whatever amount of icing you think you will need into a small bowl. Add some drops of gel food color or a toothpick swipe of paste food color and stir until the color is uniform. I like to use a butter knife to stir my icing because I feel like it incorporates less air bubbles into the icing. Some people use rubber spatulas while other people use spoons. The choice is yours. Whatever you choose, make sure that you stir slowly so you don't overmix your icing or add too much air.

It is best to color your icing before thinning it to the consistency you will be using, as some food colors will thin your icing. Also, if you are mixing three or more colors for a set of cookies, I like to add some of one color into the other colors to help them look more uniform. Typically, I will pick the brightest or darkest color and mix a pea-sized amount of that icing into the other bowls of icing. I pretty much leave white and black alone though.

Combining Cutters

1 With all the cutters that exist in the world (and in my cookie cupboard) it's hard to believe that there might be a cookie cutter that I don't have. You need a cupcake with bat wings? Or two balloons instead of one? It's often an easy fix to combine more than one cutter to get the design you want. Start by cutting out one of each cookie. In this case, two balloons.

2 Use one cutter to remove a portion of the other cutout. But before you cut, let's think ahead just a minute. You want to make the pieces as interlocking as possible, and you want your icing lines to not follow the cut lines. If the icing overlaps where the cutouts meet, it will strengthen your cookie.

3 Put the cookie pieces together on the baking sheet. Gently mush the edges together to help "glue" the cookies into each other as they bake. Allow the cookies to cool for a few minutes before moving them off the baking sheet to fully cool. You can use those minutes to admire your own ingenuity. Be aware—these combined cookies are more fragile than other cookies until they are decorated. The icing over the top of the seam creates a sturdy brace that will keep the cookie together even when being shipped.

Consistency of Icing

If I could tell you just one thing about decorating cookies, it would be to make cookies with love in your heart and don't worry so much about other people. But the second thing would be very nearly just as important. And that would be that the consistency of your icing will make or break your cookie-decorating experience. You can have the perfect cutter and the perfect cookie recipe and the perfect icing color, but if you don't take the time to get the right consistency, you will be disappointed every single time you pick up your icing bag or bottle. And disappointment leads to tears and ice cream and multiple day movie-fests. And even though I'm totally on board with the ice cream and the occasional multiple day movie-fests, let's avoid the tears, shall we?

There are four basic consistencies of icing— **thin, medium, thick** and **extra thick**. The terms are kind of self-explanatory, so let me tell you first how to make them, and then we'll talk about why and when you'll use each one.

Start by giving your icing a quick stir. See how the surface is all uneven and all of your stirring lines are just sitting there on the top? Bang the bowl on the counter five or six times. You could also tap it. (It really just depends on you and your current level of frustration.) If those lines flatten out and the surface is flat (even if you can see where the lines were, look to see if the surface is actually flat; icing likes to trick you), then you have medium icing in your bowl. If everything gets all smooth and glossy with only two taps, your icing is thin. Thick icing doesn't really settle out very well, even after tapping it seven or eight times. It's still shiny and spreadable, but will hold a soft peak if you pull the icing out of the bowl with a spoon or a knife. Extra-thick icing doesn't go anywhere. Ever. Even sometimes when you want it to. It has issues. So we don't use it very often. Extra thick icing will hold a stiff peak and has lost its shine. Maybe that's why it has issues. No shine. Poor thing.

Thin icing is also referred to as "flood icing" by many decorators. Do you know what happens with water in a flood? It goes wherever it wants to. Thin icing is the same way. It settles out quickly, so it is ideal when used to fill in a large area on a cookie, but only when that large area is cordoned off by a thicker icing. Many designs call for you to outline an area with thick icing and fill it in with thin icing. If your icing is too thin, the surface can fall on itself or you might see a lot of air bubbles in your icing.

Medium icing is sometimes referred to as "puffy icing" or "one-consistency icing" because you can outline and fill a cookie with just one consistency of icing as long as the cookie isn't large. Because it takes more time for this icing to settle out into a smooth surface, if you try to flood a large cookie with this consistency of icing, you risk the chance that it will start to dry before fully settling. Usually, I don't use this on any area larger than three inches square. Because medium icing dries faster than thin icing, it is used for a dimensional look on cookies.

Thick icing is ideal for outlining cookies and for most detail piping. It is thick enough to stay where you put it and not run all over your cookie willy-nilly. That makes it perfect for any letters or words you are thinking about putting on your cookie.

If you store your royal icing in the refrigerator, please make sure it comes to room temperature before determining how thick or thin it is. Icing gets thicker when cooled and will become substantially thinner as it warms up. So don't ruin your whole afternoon by putting your icing in a piping bag too soon and having it "melt" on you while piping. Besides, who couldn't use a few minutes to really appreciate how great life really is? Well, either that or more laundry, I suppose.

Once you figured out what consistency your icing IS and you know how thick you want it TO BE, the next step is to get it there. If your icing is too thin, sift a little powdered sugar over the top of your icing. (Do you have to sift it? No. But I will not be held responsible for lumps in your icing if you don't. That one is on you.) One tablespoon of powdered sugar is usually enough to move one cup of icing from one level of thickness to the next. If your icing is too thick, add a few drops of water. Start with three to five drops of water and test the consistency again. It takes a lot less water to thin it down than you think. Some very smart people use a spray bottle to add water instead of trying to accurately measure drops.

Cookie Cutters

Cookie cutters come in all sorts of shapes and sizes and are made with different materials. Tin cookie cutters are the most common, and usually the cheapest. They are fairly easy to bend if you want them to be thinner or taller or you could take them apart completely and reshape them into your own unique creation. Premade plastic cutters are usually in the same price range as tin cutters. I prefer these for most geometric shapes because they will not bend to your will or your magically powerful hands. Let's be honest, some of us just don't know our own strength and might accidentally reshape that perfect tin circle cutter into a lop-sided wildebeest. But with a plastic cutter, that perfect circle or square or what have you will stay exactly as it was intended to be. Printed plastic cookie cutters have that same property. They are a little more expensive than traditional plastic or tin cutters, but they can often be made to order in the exact shape and size that you request. The gold standard of cookie cutters that make angels sing are the copper cutters. They are heavier and more solid than the other types of cookie cutters. Not surprisingly, they also cost more. Copper cutters are ideal for a shape that you use a lot. They are incredibly sturdy and can cut hundreds and hundreds of cookies without breaking or reshaping themselves.

Cookie Cutters—*Make Your Own*

I love cookie cutters. They hold so much potential, so much possibility. You don't have to be an incredibly skilled decorator to own cookie cutters. But every time I look at a cutter, I think about the amazing cookies I would create if I *was* an incredibly skilled decorator. And then I buy the cookie cutter. I can't help it. How could I possibly look that cookie cutter in the eye and say, "I don't want you"? Especially when it's not true. (And also especially because they don't actually have eyes.) So I told myself to stop buying cookie cutters. But sometimes you just need a certain shape. (Like you need to eat those leftover cookies for breakfast, so that you can make more.) Since I lack the self-control to shop for just one cookie cutter or the ability to plan far enough in advance to order a cutter . . . sometimes I make my own cookie cutters!

Many cookie cutter companies sell kits to make your own cutter. It may seem daunting, but after you make just one cutter, you'll be practically an expert. Start by printing or drawing the shape you want to make. Gather random household supplies like markers, spice jars, drinking glasses, and something with a 90-degree angle corner to help you shape the cutter. Place your metal strip on a corner of your design and start bending it to fit the shape on your paper. Use the items you gathered to get smooth, even curves and perfectly straight corners. I use my hands for gentler curves and needle-nose pliers for sharper angles. If you bend it wrong the first time, just straighten the metal strip out at your mistake and try again. When you come back around to your starting point, leave about half inch of overhang and cut off the rest of the metal. Bend the overhang as necessary to fit snugly against your starting point. You can use a food safe adhesive or even double-sided tape to secure the two pieces of metal to each other. If using adhesive, make sure you give it plenty of time to dry and then wash carefully before using it the first time. No one wants adhesive in their cookie.

• •

Cookies on a Stick

There is kind of an unwritten rule in this world. If you put something on a stick, it's instantly fabulous. I mean, think about it. Remember when they had glasses on a stick? That was a real thing and those people were fabulous. Can't get your kids to eat fruits or vegetables—make them kebabs and suddenly it's their favorite food ever! Cookies on a stick are pretty much magic . . . to everyone except the cookie decorators. But with so many ways to make them, it just keeps getting easier to say YES!

You can place a stick into an unbaked cookie by placing two fingers on the bottom edge and gently sliding the stick in without morphing the cookie into unrecognizable oblivion. Or you can roll out your cookies half as thick as normal; place one on the baking sheet, put a cookie stick on top, and then cover it with another cookie. It's more work, but you have less of a chance of changing your dream cookies into nightmare shapes.

It's also possible to attach the sticks after baking and decorating. When the cookies have completely dried, you can turn them face down and pipe a thick line of thick icing on the back of the cookie. Push the cookie stick into the icing and allow it to dry completely. Or you can place the cookie in a bag and tape a stick to the back of the bag. I've found that tying ribbon around the bottom of the cookie bag and the cookie stick helps make this setup even sturdier.

• •

Cornstarch

Cornstarch can be used for a lot of things. You can dust it on top of painted cookies to "set" the food color so it won't bleed or rub off on the package. Some people replace up to a half cup of the flour in a cookie dough recipe with cornstarch to soften the bite of their cookies. If added to royal icing, cornstarch makes the icing crunchier.

• •

Corn Syrup

Corn syrup is sometimes added when making royal icing to make the icing softer. The cookies are still solid enough to stack, but the corn syrup takes out the crunch of the royal icing. (This is especially helpful if your powdered sugar has cornstarch in it.) Try using one tablespoon of corn syrup for every two pounds of powdered sugar in your recipe. Add even more corn syrup to the icing when you plan to make it extra-thick consistency.

Corn syrup can also be brushed onto an iced cookie that is completely dry. Brush it on smooth and let it dry completely (up to twenty-four hours) for an incredibly shiny surface. Or, mix two parts corn syrup with one part water to create a sugary "glue" for edible images, glitter dust, or sanding sugars.

Couplers

A decorating coupler is made of two pieces of plastic—the base and the ring. The base fits inside the decorating bag, with the narrow end going in first. If using a bottle, the bottle coupler base is first screwed onto the bottle. A decorating tip is placed on top of the base from the outside of the piping bag or bottle. The ring part of the coupler slides down over the decorating tip and screws to the base. The coupler allows you to change decorating tips as often as you like without changing the icing in the bag or bottle.

Not all couplers are created equally. Wilton makes their couplers with a notch in the base to allow for their drop flower tips. This notch sometimes interferes with how well it connects to the ring and if you cross-thread the ring and coupler, icing can squeeze out when you're not looking and fall like tears on to your now-ruined cookie. I highly recommend Ateco couplers. They attach securely every time.

Craters

Sometimes the surface of the icing isn't strong enough to hold air trapped underneath it and craters or dents will form. You can sometimes cover a crater or dent with a flower or bow or other extra unplanned adornment. There are also a few things you can do to help avoid craters. Use the thickest possible icing consistency for the design you are working on. If you aren't using fresh icing, use a hand mixer to whip the icing for thirty seconds to help it hold up again. If you are filling a tiny space, it can help to run a toothpick or scriber through the icing before it dries. And once you have piped the icing on the cookie, use a moving air source (standing fan or dehydrator) to dry the top layer of the icing as quickly as possible.

Cupcake

 Use a cupcake cutter to cut out cookies, and then bake them according to recipe directions.

2 Outline and fill the wrapper portion of the cupcake with medium-consistency blue icing and a #3 tip. Let it dry for 15 minutes.

3 With medium-consistency yellow icing and a #3 tip, add a little strip of icing above the blue icing. Let it dry for 15 minutes.

4 This is my favorite part. With medium-consistency white icing and a #3 tip, add the bottom layer of swirl right above the yellow icing. Let it dry for 5–10 minutes.

5 Add another layer of swirl above the first and let it dry for 5 minutes or until the surface is set.

6 Add the final dollop of white icing at the top of the cupcake. Resist the urge to bury your face in the icing.

7 Use blue food color markers to make wrapper lines on the blue icing. Alternatively, you could paint those lines on with blue food coloring and a food grade paintbrush.

8 Add a red stripe across the wrapper with medium-consistency red icing and a #3 tip.

9 Before the red icing dries, add a **Royal Icing Transfer** circle on top of the red line. Press gently into the red icing to secure it.

10 Use a food color marker to write the age or an initial on the white circle. Use the **Vintage** painting technique to age the cookie, if you like.

Disposable Icing Bag

Disposable icing bags are made of thick or thin clear plastic. They are intended to be used once and then thrown away. The thicker bags made by Wilton can be washed and reused multiple times. The thinner bags are really just for a one time use. These are great for decorating parties, for people who don't have a lot of time for extra clean-up, and for any time you want to be able to quickly see the color of the icing in a bag. Ebay is a fantastic place to get good deals on disposable bags, although more cookie decorating supply stores are starting to carry these as well. To use, place the tip of the icing bag in a small drinking glass. Fold the edges of the bag over the cup. Spoon icing into the bag. Bring the edges up and seal by tying a knot, or using a bag clip or a rubber band. Use scissors to cut an opening in the tip of the bag. Cut a smaller hole than you think you need because you can't uncut that piping bag. If you do happen to need a smaller hole than you cut, you can slip the entire piping bag into another disposable bag and try again.

Dog

1 Use a onesie cutter to cut out cookies, and then bake them according to recipe directions.

2 With medium-consistency brown icing, outline and fill face area on the cookie. Let it dry for 30 minutes before continuing to the next step.

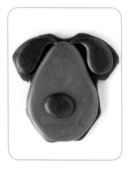

3 Pipe a small oval in the middle of the face for the nose with medium-consistency black icing and a #3 tip. Pipe ears with the same icing.

4 Use medium-consistency icing to pipe two small white dots for eyes. Immediately add two smaller black dots on top. With thick black icing and a #1.5 tip, add eyebrows and a mouth.

Double Heart

1 Use a heart cutter to combine two hearts into one cookie before baking. See **Combining Cutters** for more help.

2 This step is optional. Fill the entire cookie with medium-consistency white icing. Allow to dry overnight. If you choose not to do this step, make sure that your gray lines cover both sides of the seams where the two hearts are connected.

3 Use medium-consistency gray icing and a #3 tip to pipe a heart shape on the left cookie. Leave a space the same width as your line in the right side of the heart for the second heart to pass through. Allow to dry for 15 minutes.

4 Pipe the second heart on the right side of the cookie. Use a toothpick to completely fill in the gap that was left in the first heart if necessary.

5 Pipe a small square of medium-consistency pink icing over the bottom seam of the hearts. Let it dry for at least 15 minutes.

6 Add ribbons to either side of the pink square with the same icing.

Drying Cookies

Decorated cookies take up to twenty-four hours to dry completely. The surface of icing will usually crust over and appear dry within the first thirty minutes, so it can sometimes be difficult to know when they are dry. To avoid damage to your cookies, do not cover or stack them for at least twenty-four hours. To speed drying times, use a moving air source to wick moisture away as it evaporates. Many people use standing fans, heater fans, heat guns, or dehydrators to help speed this process. To avoid the risk of also drying out the cookie, leave the moving air on the cookies for only the first thirty minutes of drying time. (This time can be extended if you live in a very humid climate.) The added advantage of using moving air to help dry your cookies is that the moving air will also add a small shine to your icing as it dries. Another alternative to speed drying times is to warm the decorated cookies slightly so the water from the icing evaporates into the air faster. Some people use the light of their oven or other mobile light to accomplish this. Be careful not to heat your cookies above 90 degrees or the icing can discolor or wrinkle.

Dusts

There are a jillion different kinds of dusts. And it seems like every company that makes them calls them by a different name. It can get confusing. Petal dusts have a matte finish. You can get a veritable rainbow of petal dusts. They come in loose powder or pressed tiles. Petal dusts will leave a deep or saturated color on your dry icing. Luster, pearl, and shimmer dusts are colored dusts that are shiny. They come in metallic colors like silver, gold, and bronze and also basic colors like pink and blue. Although these colors may look dark, the color they leave on the dry icing, while shimmery, is muted. Sparkle dust is like luster dust but with a visible texture. Twinkle, disco, and pixie dusts are the next step up in coarseness. They are like tiny little pieces of nontoxic glitter. They will not color your icing at all.

Use a food-grade paintbrush to paint these dusts onto your dried icing. Petal and luster dusts can be applied dry or wet. To brush on wet, mix a small amount of the dust with water or lemon extract. You can mix it in a small bowl or the lid of the dust. If you use a dish, leave the extra in there and when the liquid evaporates, you can brush it back into the container. If using the lid, just put it back on when it's dry. If you are brushing a large quantity of dust onto your cookie, you can set the color by passing the cookie through the steam of boiling water. These dusts are perfect for highlighting details like pink cheeks and shine lines on snowmen.

Disco dusts are easier to apply by sprinkling over a wet layer of icing. You can either sprinkle them onto the icing before it dries or brush water or corn syrup where you want the disco dust after the icing has fully dried. Just a tip—these little jars can be tricky to open. Use a flat-ended bottle opener to easily remove the lid without spilling all that precious dust over every inch of your kitchen.

Edible Images

An edible image is a sheet of frosting "paper" that has been printed on with food coloring. There are specific printers for this, or you can buy a brand-new printer (that has never used real ink) that is compatible with the food coloring cartridges. Alternatively, check with local bakeries. Many of them will print the images you need for a fee. The frosting sheets are soft when printed. It is best to let them sit in the air for ten to fifteen minutes to harden just enough to peel the frosting off the protective plastic backing without tearing the frosting sheet. If you let it sit out for more than twenty minutes, though, the frosting sheet will become brittle and will crack when you try to remove it. So if you aren't going to use it right away, keep it in a large airtight bag. Edible images are a great way to re-create something exactly—like portraits and logos—without spending your entire life on them. To apply the edible images, first cut around the image. Be aware that the edges will be visible when placed on the cookie. So plan to cover them with a piped border or make sure you cut them just how you want them to appear. You can put the image directly onto wet icing or wait until the icing dries and then paint the surface of the cookie with corn syrup before applying the image. The frosting sheet can wrinkle if the icing underneath is too thin or if you apply too much corn syrup. Also, dark colors of icing can bleed through the white areas of edible images.

Emulsions and Extracts

Emulsions and extracts come in more flavors than you can imagine. They can both be added to either cookie dough or icing. They are used in equal amounts—so if a recipe calls for one teaspoon extract, you can use one teaspoon emulsion instead. An extract is a flavor diluted in alcohol. Extracts are either pure or imitation and imitation extracts are usually clear. An emulsion is a flavor suspended in a mix of water and vegetable gum. Alcohol evaporates fairly quickly at room temperature. You can only imagine how quickly it's going to take off in the heat of an oven. And when it goes, it takes some of its flavor friends with it. Because of this, more of an extract flavor is "baked out" than that of an emulsion. And just so you know, those "candy oils" are actually the concentrated flavors with no dilution. They can also be used in cookie dough or even royal icing. Usually three to four drops will be all you need. When adding candy oils to royal icing, make sure you add them at the very end when the icing is already mixed.

Eyeballs

Eyeballs can be piped directly onto cookies or onto waxed or parchment paper to be saved for a later use. You can make them as simple as black dots on a white circle, or detailed with light glinting off the iris. Whatever you choose, make sure you have all colors ready to go before you start piping the first step. All colors are piped directly onto wet icing to create a smooth eyeball.

1. Use medium-consistency white icing and a #3 tip to pipe small dots of white. If you are making eyeballs to use later, don't pipe more than 10–15 eyes at a time or they will start to dry before you can move to the next step.

2. With medium-consistency green (or blue or brown) icing, add smaller dots to the center of the eyes. If you want to make simple eyes, you can use black here instead of green and then call it a day.

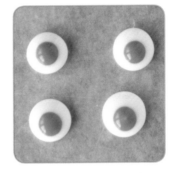

3. Add even smaller dots of black on top of the green. Use a scriber or toothpick if necessary to smooth the center of the black icing.

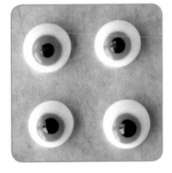

4. Use a toothpick or scriber to add the tiniest amount of white icing to the eye where the black and green icings meet. Let the eyes dry for at least an hour before removing them from the waxed or parchment paper.

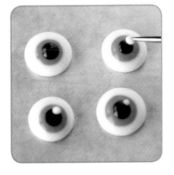

Eyes

1 Sometimes a more realistic eye is desired. With a #1 tip or a food grade paintbrush, fill a small area of the face with thin white icing.

2 Pipe a colored dot of icing on both white areas. Immediately add a black dot on top and a much smaller white dot where the black and colored icing meet.

3 Use a #1.5 tip and thick black icing to outline the top of the eye.

4 With medium-consistency skin-colored icing, outline the face area. Then outline the eye. Fill in the face area with the same icing, being careful to not overfill the area around the eyes.

5 Finish decorating the face as desired.

 F

Flowers in a Jar

1 Combine a mason jar cutter and a clover cutter before baking. See **Combining Cutters** for more help.

2 Outline and fill the jar part of the cookie with medium-consistency blue icing and a #3 tip. Immediately add flower stems with medium-consistency green icing and a #3 tip. Use a smaller tip for thinner stems. Allow to dry for 1–2 hours.

3 Use medium-consistency white icing and a #3 tip to outline and fill the flower portion of the cookie. Immediately add flower stems with the same green icing as before. Let dry for 30 minutes.

4 Outline flower shapes with thick pink icing and a #3 tip. Use the white icing from before to pipe a tag on the jar part of the cookie.

5 This step requires you to work fast. Fill in the flowers with medium-consistency light-pink icing. Immediately add scalloped lines with thick pink icing and a #2 tip. Drop some white nonpareils in the center of the flowers.

6 With thick blue icing and a #3 tip, add jar detail lines.

7 Add vegetation to the bouquet by piping first a center line with medium green icing and a #2 tip. Add dots for leaves along either side. Pipe a small heart on the tag and, with thick gray icing and a #1.5 tip, add a string around the jar's top and to the tag.

Fondant

Fondant is kind of like a grown-up version of play dough. You can mold it and shape it and roll it out flat or use it to make 3-D decorations like flowers or bows. If you are using it as a base layer for your cookie instead of flooding it, roll out the fondant as the cookies are baking and cut the fondant with the same cookie cutter. When the cookies come out of the oven, place the fondant pieces on top while the cookies are still warm. If you miss that window because you are actually living your life while baking cookies, you can also brush a cool cookie with corn syrup or water and place the fondant on top as well.

Fondant should be stored in an airtight container at room temperature when not in use. You have about fifteen minutes to use your pieces of fondant before they will start cracking when bent. If you want to cut them out ahead of time, you can layer them between sheets of waxed paper in an airtight container. If you are using fondant for dimensional decorations, you will probably want them to dry out before placing them on the cookies. When cookies with fondant decorations are put in an airtight container (or bag) the fondant will absorb some of the moisture from the cookies and "melt" a little bit. Because of this, dimensional fondant decorations are not suitable for shipping on cookies. There are many different kinds of fondant. This is a quick recipe for fondant that doesn't taste like chemicals and uses ingredients you probably already have in your kitchen.

Ingredients:

1 (16-oz.) bag mini marshmallows

2 Tbsp. water

2 tsp. corn syrup

2 tsp. lemon juice

½ tsp. salt

2 tsp. vanilla flavor

1 (2-lb.) bag powdered sugar

Spray a microwave safe bowl with nonstick pan spray. Pour the marshmallows and water into the bowl. Microwave for 2 minutes or so. (Every microwave is different.) Stir after 90 seconds. It should be soupy when it is fully melted.

If you are going to use a stand mixer, spray your bowl with nonstick spray and pour the whole soupy mess in now. Add corn syrup, lemon juice, salt, and vanilla. Stir well. Using a dough hook, add the powdered sugar 1 cup at a time. If you are mixing by hand, it is absolutely imperative that you sift the sugar first. (And I'm a non-sifter, so trust me on this one.)

Watch the mixer carefully. As soon as the fondant is thick enough to hold a shape, stop mixing it. If you touch it with your finger, it should be soft and feel tacky, but it shouldn't stick to you like some other-worldly creature that wants to steal your life force. Humidity will change the exact amount of powdered sugar you need to add every time for the perfect consistency. You'll get the hang of it.

. . . .

Food Color Markers

Just like they sound, food markers are markers that are filled with food coloring instead of ink. They can be used to sketch designs on a cookie before starting or for finishing details. You can flood an entire cookie in white and draw the entire design with food color markers, or let children "color" their own cookies. Food color makers should be stored tip down. They can be "recharged" by removing the cap on the bottom of the marker and soaking the foam core in food coloring overnight. They come in different styles from bold to fine point. They typically come as an assortment, although you can also buy black on its own.

. . . .

Food Coloring

Food coloring is sold as a liquid, a paste, a gel, and even in a powdered form. Liquid food coloring is usually heavily diluted in water and is not suitable for cookie decorating. The efficacy of powdered food color depends on the brand and type. Most natural food colors are powdered. Paste and gel food coloring are both heavily concentrated. Paste food coloring is sold in a pot or jar and requires a knife or toothpick to use while gel food coloring comes in a bottle and can be squeezed out into the icing. I prefer gel food coloring because it's easy to use while still being concentrated enough to not change the consistency of my icing very much. Food coloring doesn't taste good on its own and can stain skin and clothing. Be careful when using it. If you do get it on your skin, I have found that a mix of baking soda, salt, and a little water does an amazing job of getting it off.

Fox

1 Use a ring cutter to cut out cookies, and then bake them according to recipe directions.

2 Use medium-consistency cream-colored icing and a #3 tip to outline and fill a triangle shape for the head. Let it dry for at least 15 minutes.

3 I don't really have words for the shape that you need to pipe next. Just use the same icing and outline and fill the tummy section. Let it dry for 1 hour to avoid color bleed.

4 Fill in the sides with medium-consistency copper-colored icing.

5 Pipe over the head with the same copper-colored icing, leaving large patches open around the eyes.

6 Pipe upside down "v" shapes for the ears and fill with the cream-colored icing. Pipe a tail with the copper icing and a #3 tip. Let dry for 15 minutes.

7 Use thick black icing and a #1.5 tip to add eyes, a nose, and a black tip to the tail. Use luster dust or pink food coloring and a food grade paintbrush to add pink to the cheeks.

Frame

1 Use a fancy plaque cutter to cut out frame cookies. Before baking, use a small oval cutter to make an impression on each cutout. Bake according to recipe directions.

2 With medium-consistency white icing and a #3 tip, outline and fill center of frame. Let it dry for an hour to avoid color bleed.

3 I use extra-thick black icing for the frame part of this cookie. Remember to add some corn syrup to the icing before thickening it with powdered sugar to keep it from getting extra crunchy. The key to this frame is to keep everything symmetrical. Whatever you do on one side, repeat it on the other. Pipe a small dot at the top and bottom of the frame. Add lines from each dot that meet on both sides.

4 Put a #16 star tip on your piping bag. Pipe two teardrops at the top of the frame and two at the bottom. Basically, you are going to squeeze like you are making a dot of icing and then pull the tip toward the frame to complete the shape.

5 Pipe an "e" shape to the right of the teardrops on the top of the frame. Mirror that motion on the other side and then flip it for the bottom loops.

6 Pipe a line starting at the swirls you just made, follow the curve of the frame, and finish with another swirl just like the first ones.

7 Finish the frame with more "e" shapes or swirls on both sides of the frame. It's okay if it's not perfect. There are details all over the place on this cookie that will keep your eyes busy. No one is going to be judging your symmetry. Let the cookie dry for at least 30 minutes.

8 Use silver airbrush paint to add texture to the frame.

9 Add ROYAL ICING TRANSFERS to the center of the frame, or pipe the design of your choice.

Freezing

If you are thinking about it, you can probably freeze it—from cookie dough to decorated cookies. Cookie dough can be frozen for up to four months in a sealed container. You can also freeze cutouts before baking. It's best to freeze cutouts in a single layer and then transfer them to an airtight container once frozen. Layer them with waxed paper and they will also keep for up to four months in the freezer. There is no need to thaw frozen cutouts before baking. Just place them on your baking sheet and add an additional minute or two of baking time.

Royal icing and glaze can also be frozen for three to four months. Place them in a sealed container to keep them from tasting like your freezer. When you are ready to use them, let them come to room temperature, then stir them both thoroughly, making sure to incorporate the thicker sugar layer on the bottom. Royal icing will sometimes need to be refreshed with an electric mixer on high for thirty seconds.

To freeze undecorated cookies, allow them to cool completely after baking. Layer them between waxed paper in an airtight container. You can keep them in the freezer for four to six weeks before decorating. Make sure they are at room temperature before decorating. And the biggest surprise of all—you can also freeze decorated cookies. Allow decorated cookies to dry for at least twelve hours. Place them in a ziplock plastic bag inside an airtight container. If you aren't confident the icing is completely dry, you can layer them between waxed paper as well. I've frozen decorated cookies for up to three months with no noticeable change in flavor or texture and no change to the icing. For health concerns, it should be noted that the cookie dough should only be frozen once. If you thaw it, you should bake the cookies or throw it away. The baked cookies can be frozen even if they came from previously frozen cookie dough. But, again, you should only freeze and thaw the baked cookies one time.

Gift

1 Use a gift cutter to cut out cookies, and then bake them according to recipe directions.

2 Use thick blue icing to outline the bottom portion of the gift.

3 Use thin blue icing to fill the space inside your outline. Immediately add dots of medium-consistency white icing to create a polka-dot pattern. Allow to dry for 1 hour.

4 Add a ribbon with medium-consistency white icing and a #3 tip.

5 Use thick red icing and a #3 tip to outline the bow. I think it is easiest to pipe the top teardrop shape first, and then outline the rest of it. Let it dry for 15 minutes.

6 Fill in the bow area with medium-consistency red icing and a #2 tip.

7 Add a dot between the bows with the same red icing.

8 You could leave it all shiny and new if you want. Or you can make it vintage with the **Vintage** painting technique.

Gingerbread Cookies

Traditional gingerbread cookies require 3–4 hours of chilling in the refrigerator. These chewy gingerbread cookies don't need any time to chill. They have a mellow flavor and won't spread.

Ingredients:

1 cup butter

1½ cups brown sugar

2 large eggs

⅓ cup molasses

1 Tbsp. cinnamon

2 tsp. allspice

1 tsp. ginger

½ tsp. salt

4–4½ cups flour

Cream butter and sugar together. Add eggs and molasses and mix well. Stir in the spices and salt all at once. Add the flour 1 cup at a time. Add only as much as you need to be able to roll out the dough, and then cut your fancy little shapes of perfection. If, by chance, you are planning on taking some leisure time to yourself and want to wait to bake these cookies, go ahead and stop adding flour at 4 cups. The dough will dry up a bit as the flour absorbs more of the molasses. Roll out on a lightly floured surface. I roll my cookies to about ¼-inch thick and bake them at 375 degrees for 7 minutes. If you roll to ⅜-inch thick, bake them for 10 minutes.

Giraffe

1 Use a bell cutter to cut out cookies, and then bake them according to recipe directions. If necessary, cut the top handle off the bell before baking.

2 Turn the bell upside down. Outline and fill a small section of what is now the bottom of the cookie with medium-consistency cream icing and a #3 tip. Allow to dry for at least 15 minutes.

3 Outline and fill the rest of the face with medium-consistency yellow icing and a #3 tip.

4 Outline ears with yellow icing and immediately fill with cream icing.

5 Pipe two small ovals for eyes with white icing and immediately add two much smaller black dots on top. Use the same yellow icing to pipe two small horns. Begin by piping a dot at the top and then use the decorating tip to drag the icing toward the head.

6 Add brown patterns with medium brown icing and a #1.5 tip. Add nostrils with the same icing and tip.

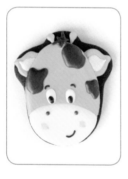

7 Add a crop of hair at the top with the medium brown icing and #1.5 tip. With thick black icing and a #1.5 tip, add eyebrows and a mouth. Use pink luster dust or food coloring to paint the cheeks.

· ·

Glaze Icing

All of the cookies in this book are made with royal icing. Precise details and dimension are more difficult to achieve with glaze than with royal icing.

That doesn't mean you can't still make beautiful cookies with glaze. Glaze just works differently than royal icing and dries softer. I use royal icing because that's what I'm used to. If you can't stand the thought of royal icing, or just want to be adventurous, give this basic glaze recipe a try.

Ingredients:

2 pounds powdered sugar

½ cup water

½ cup corn syrup

2 tsp. vanilla extract

Place all ingredients in a bowl and mix on low speed until smooth.

Halloween (See *Candelabra*, *Cat*, *Frame*, *Pumpkin*, and *Ruffle Pumpkin*)

Hand Cutting Cookies (See also *Cookie Cutters* and *Cookie Cutters—Make Your Own*)

I think there might be more cookie cutters than people in the world. But even with all those different cutters in existence, there will always be shapes you want to bake that you don't have a cutter for. If you only need one or two of them, hand cutting will be your best friend. Start by drawing or printing your shape on a piece of paper. Very carefully cut the shape out exactly as you want it. Spray the paper with nonstick spray or rub both sides with vegetable oil. This will strengthen the paper and also help it stay on the cookie dough without actually sticking to it. Roll out your cookie dough and chill it for fifteen to twenty minutes. Place your template on the surface of your cookie dough and smooth it gently to adhere it to the surface. Use a small, sharp knife—like a paring knife—to make small vertical cuts around the edge of your template. When you have finished cutting out your shape, use a spatula to lift the cutout with the template still attached. Rub your finger around the edges to get rid of any rough edges. Transfer to a baking sheet, remove the template, and bake as normal.

Kissing Lips

1 Use a folk heart cutter to cut out cookies and then bake them according to recipe directions.

2 Turn the heart on its side. Use a medium-consistency pink icing and a #3 tip to outline and fill what is now the bottom portion of the lip. While the icing is still wet, immediately add a drop of white icing to the lip. Use a toothpick or scriber to drag white drop into a shine line. Allow to dry for 15 minutes.

3 Repeat the same process for the top lip. Let the entire cookie dry for 4 hours or overnight if you live in a humid environment.

4 Fill in the teeth section of the cookie with medium-consistency white icing. You can use a toothpick or scriber to help pull the white icing back into that small area where the lips meet.

Kopykake

A Kopykake is a projector that uses lightbulbs and a mirror to project a printed image down on to the surface of your cookie. You then are able to "trace" the image with your icing. It allows you to accurately re-create fonts, shapes, and even your own drawings. There are two models of Kopykake projectors, commonly abbreviated as a KK. The 300XK is the more common of the two. It is the cheapest option and comes with only one 250-watt lightbulb. (Replacements can be found at most hardware stores. Pick up an extra one; they burn out when you most need them.) Because it only has one lightbulb, the image can be difficult to see if the room lights are also on. The K1000 solved this problem with two lightbulbs, and a higher price. Both projectors allow you to scale your printed images up to 300 percent larger, but they aren't as good at scaling the images down. It is best to print your images the same size you want them, or slightly smaller.

Some people find it hard to pipe while using a KK because their hand gets in the way of the projected image. Remember, you can rotate the KK sideways or even trace the image with a food marker and then pipe over your lines later.

Lettering

Adding words to a cookie can be a frustrating experience, but it doesn't have to be. There are so many lovely fonts and handwritten words that are easily re-created in icing with a few simple tricks. First, make sure you have the right consistency of icing. You need a thick consistency of icing for letters that won't blend together. Make sure your icing will hold a soft peak before placing it in your piping bag or bottle. Use a small tip for small letters. I actually prefer to use a disposable icing bag for lettering because I can cut the smallest hole that ever existed and have complete control over my icing. Other people use PME tips #0 or #00 for lettering. If you have a naturally flowing handwriting, throw caution to the wind and just pipe those words on the cookie. If you "have issues with perfection" or just prefer to be cautious, you can use a Kopykake projector to get evenly spaced letters. You can also print out the desired font and slip it into a sheet protector and practice with the icing a few times before trying it on a cookie. Some people have also found it helpful to write the words on the cookie first with a food color marker and then pipe over the top of the marker. I've also found that when you are piping a word, it is helpful to leave off all the crossbars and hooks and curly parts until the end. Then come back and fill them in. It gives the original part of the letter just barely enough time to form a super thin crust so the two parts don't join forces and create a tidal wave of melting letter destruction on your cookie.

Meringue Powder

Royal icing was originally made with raw egg whites. Since raw eggs have that whole "how much do you value your life?" thing going on, some pretty smart people came up with the idea to pasteurize egg whites and sell them in powder form so they would be safe to consume without cooking. You can buy straight powdered egg whites, or you can buy them mixed with a little sugar and cornstarch and sometimes other proprietary ingredients. This mix is called meringue powder. You should be able to find it at most baking and craft stores that have a cake decorating section. In addition to royal icing, meringue powder can also be used for—surprise!!—making actual meringue or to help stabilize buttercream icing on those hot summer days. You can also make those delicious little meringue cookies with it. You know, in case of a meringue cookie emergency.

Mermaid

1 Use a rubber duck cutter to cut out cookies, and bake them according to recipe directions.

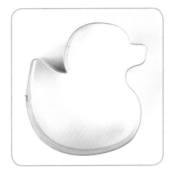

2 Turn the cookie upside down. Use medium-consistency skin-colored icing to pipe a face in the middle of the cookie. You can make it a circle if you want. I prefer heart-shaped faces. This one is your call though.

3 With medium-consistency blue icing and a #3 tip, outline and fill the fin. Immediately sprinkle with blue sanding sugar. Let it dry for 30 minutes before removing excess sanding sugar.

4 Add a torso and neck with the skin-colored icing. Let it dry for 15 minutes or until set.

5 Let's give this girl some arms.

6 Add 2 green dots of icing to the torso. Use the decorating tip to drag them toward her arms. Outline and fill the hair with medium-consistency pink icing and a #3 tip.

7 Pipe two small eyes with thick black icing and a #1.5 tip. Add pink cheeks using luster dust (or food coloring) and a food grade paintbrush. Add hair details with thick pink icing and a #2 tip.

Molds

If you want to use molds for cookies, first make sure that you have a non-spreading cookie dough recipe. (See **Chocolate Sugar Cookie** or **Vanilla Sugar Cookie** for two great options.) Follow the instructions on the mold to prepare it for use by either dusting with cornstarch or spraying with nonstick oil. Push the cookie dough into the mold and use a knife to cut off the excess cookie dough. Chill in the refrigerator for three to five minutes before releasing the dough from the mold. Place the dough on a baking sheet and repeat until you have enough cookies to bake. When the cookies come out of the oven, they will look puffy, but will settle into the molded design as they cool. Molds are also great with fondant or melting chocolate to add dimensions and decorations on top of cookies. Silicone molds are the easiest to use, but plastic and ceramic molds are also available.

Monkey

1 Use the paw cutter to cut out cookies. Use a sharp knife to smooth the top before baking.

2 Turn the cookies so the knobby places are on the bottom. Use medium-consistency cream icing and a #3 tip to outline and fill in the face. Let it dry for 20 minutes.

3 With medium-consistency brown icing and a #3 tip, pipe around the face to create the head.

4 Outline ears with the same brown icing and immediately fill with the cream icing.

5 Use thick black icing and a #1.5 tip to add eyes, nose, and mouth. Use pink luster dust or food coloring to add pink cheeks.

6 You can make it a girl by adding bigger eyes and a flower above the ear.

Oil and Royal Icing

Once upon a time, long ago, in a land far away, a wise old woman tried to make royal icing and failed because there was a tiny speck of oil in her icing bowl. So she washed and washed and washed that bowl. She wiped it with vinegar to completely remove all traces of that fat. And then she tried again and was wildly successful and saved the kingdom from ruin. Most people who work with royal icing have heard this story or, admittedly, a less fairy-tale version of it. The truth is, even the tiniest speck of oil can keep your egg whites from reaching soft peak stage and ruin your icing . . . but only if you are using fresh egg whites. If you are using meringue powder or powdered egg whites, it will take a lot more than a speck of oil to ruin your icing. I know because one time I put oil on a paper towel and wiped my entire mixing bowl with it and still made perfect royal icing. When I went all out and buttered my bowl, well . . . that was a different story. Do you want to know what happened when I added butter to my royal icing after it was mixed? I got butter-flavored royal icing that didn't dry as hard. So fat is only an enemy to royal icing before the eggs are whipped, and even trace amounts are okay before that when you are using egg in powdered forms.

Outlining

The key to a perfectly smooth outline that never gets overrun with icing is a #3 tip that doesn't touch the cookie. Well, it does when you start. See, here's the deal—everyone shakes. If you breathe, you move. If you think, you move. It happens. Work with it. Touch your tip to the cookie as you begin to outline. Gently bring the tip up above the cookie about half an inch and think about laying the icing down on the edge of the cookie as if it were a string of yarn. The icing comes out smooth and lays down smooth. The #3 tip gives you enough height on the edge of the cookie so you can completely fill the space in the middle with icing and not worry about it overflowing the wall you just built around the outside edge. You can use either medium or thick icing to pipe the outline. Extra thick icing will hurt your hands trying to pipe it smoothly and can fall off the cookie when dry.

Pacifier

1 Round out the bottom part of the ornament cutter before cutting. Or use a circle cutter or the side of the ornament cutter itself. Just hold it at an angle you so don't cut the rest of the cookie at the same time. Bake according to recipe directions.

2 This step is optional. Outline and fill the entire cookie with white icing. Allow it to dry for several hours.

3 Pipe a blob that vaguely resembles a keyhole with medium-consistency tan icing and a #3 tip. Let it dry for 15 minutes.

4 Pipe an oval around the nipple with medium-consistency green icing. While the icing is still wet, add 2 drops of white icing on either side.

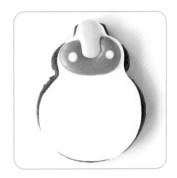

5 Use thick taupe icing and a #3 tip to pipe a ring for the pacifier.

Packaging

Packaging isn't always necessary. Cookies are meant to be eaten, and often that happens right away. Or maybe you made the cookies for a special event and putting them on a simple platter is the perfect presentation. Even when packaging isn't essential to the destiny of your cookies, dressing them up a little can make them feel like the fabulous treasures they are and keep them at their freshest for as long as possible.

If you are intending to give the cookies away on a platter, try using faux crystal plates from party or dollar stores. They come in square, oval, and circle shapes. They are also available in black, white, or metallic in addition to the crystal. Scrunch up some plastic wrap and lay it on the platter before placing cookies on top to keep them from sliding around. You can cover the platter with more plastic wrap or buy extra-large bags (also known as basket bags) and tie them with ribbon.

You can also wrap them individually in cellophane bags. Cellophane bags come in many thicknesses, but for cookies you should get something between 1.2–1.6 millimeters to keep the cookies fresh. There are three options for sealing the bags—use self-sealing bags (sometimes called lip and tape), tie them with coordinating ribbon, or use an impulse sealer to quickly seal the bag with heat.

Painting

1 Did you know that you can paint on cookies with food coloring? It's super easy and opens a whole new world of design possibilities. Paint palettes are available at most craft stores and online at very low prices. You can get palettes with as few as six wells or palettes with more than forty wells. For best possible color control, set your palette up two to three hours before painting so the food coloring will dry. Place a drop or two of the food coloring of your choice into each well. If you are pressed for time, you can still use fresh food coloring; just be careful that you don't get too much on your brush at a time.

2 You can use any food grade brush you like. My favorites are rounded brushes, tiny spotter brushes, and flat brushes. Dip the brush in water and then gently blot it on a paper towel. It should not be dripping. Rub it over the dry food coloring to release some of the color.

3 And then start painting! If you want lighter color or smaller lines, clean the brush and slightly dry it on paper towels before dipping it in the released (wet) color. If you are going to paint large swatches of your cookie like in this picture, just dip your whole brush in the released color and go for it.

4 If you make a mistake, clean and dry your brush. Use the brush to wipe the food coloring off the cookie, wiping it on a paper towel to keep it clean.

5 You can paint your life away on cookies. It's so fun. I can't stop myself sometimes. I might have a painting problem. Just remember to use the smallest amount of water you can get away with. The surface should dry within 30 seconds of painting. If your food coloring is more watered down than that, the water will start to dissolve the surface of the royal icing.

Palm Trees

1 Use a palm tree cutter to cut out cookies, and then bake them according to recipe directions. Don't be afraid to bend your cutters so they look better. Every palm tree cutter I have found is flat on top. I just pulled the leaves up and out to make it look fuller.

2 Outline and fill the trunk portion of the cookie with medium-consistency light-brown icing and a #3 tip. Immediately add some zigzag lines with medium-consistency dark-brown icing and a #2 tip.

3 Outline and fill the leaf section with medium-consistency green icing and a #3 tip. Let it dry for 15 minutes.

4 Add detail lines with thick lighter-green icing and a #2 tip.

Piping Bag

Made of plastic, vinyl, or silicone, piping bags look like empty ice cream cones. Before using them, you will need to cut the tip off to fit a coupler. Slide the base part of a coupler into the new piping bag, narrow end first. Press it in firmly and then mark where it presses against the piping bag. Pull the base of the coupler out, and use sharp kitchen scissors to cut across the tip of the piping bag on the mark. You are now ready to use your piping bag!

Slide the base of the coupler into the bag until it is snug against the opening. Place a decorating tip on top, and slide the ring of the coupler over the decorating tip. Attach the ring firmly, but be careful not to overtighten. Place the tip of the piping bag into a short drinking glass and fold the outside edges of the piping bag over the rim of the glass. Now you can pour or spoon your icing into the piping bag with both hands. Thank goodness.

When your icing is all loaded up and ready to go, unfold the edges from the rim of the glass and gather together in a twist. You can keep the icing from coming out by folding the piping bag at the twist and setting it back in the glass. Or you can put a culinary rubber band around the bag. My very favorite option is to use a bag clip. It will even keep the icing in when little hands squeeze all willy-nilly.

· ·

Piping Tips

These small metal (or plastic) cones have shaped openings to produce different shapes and textures as the icing moves from the icing bag through the piping tip. The most common cookie decorating tips are the sizes #1–3, all of which are simple circle shapes. There are many other very useful tips for making leaves, flowers, grass, ribbons, and so on. Wilton, Ateco, and PME are the most easily found brands. The tip numbers from each company are generally the same for the circle tips with small variances in sizes, but can be different for the other shapes. I use PME tips in this book unless otherwise noted.

· ·

Pumpkin

1 Use a pumpkin cutter to cut out cookies, and then bake them according to recipe directions.

2 With medium-consistency orange icing and a #3 tip, outline and fill an elongated teardrop shape in the center of the pumpkin.

3 Outline and fill sections of similar width along the edges of the pumpkin. Let dry for at least 30 minutes.

4 Fill the sections in the middle with the same icing.

5 Add a stem with medium-consistency green icing and a #2 tip. When making green icing for pumpkins, I always add some of the orange icing to the green so that the two colors coordinate better.

Recipes (See *Chocolate Sugar Cookies, Fondant, Gingerbread Cookies, Glaze, Royal Icing with Meringue Powder, Royal Icing with Powdered Egg Whites,* and *Vanilla Sugar Cookies*)

Reindeer

1 Use a snowman cutter to cut out cookies, and then bake them according to recipe directions.

2 Turn the cookie upside down. With a medium-consistency brown icing and a #3 tip, pipe what appears to be an egg with a bite taken out of the top. It was probably a chocolate candy egg. Let it dry for 15 minutes.

3 Pipe another egg-shaped blob on top of the first one. This time it's upside down and will magically turn into a head. Give it a few minutes for the surface to set before moving on.

4 Add two tiny brown ears at the top of the head. I find it easiest to pipe a circle where the top of the ear will be and then use my icing tip to drag the dot toward the head. Immediately repeat the process with medium-consistency white icing before the brown has time to dry.

5 Pipe some fancy reindeer antlers with the same brown icing and #3 tip. You could also do plain and comfy reindeer antlers for those days where your reindeer just doesn't feel like going out. It's up to you. I don't judge.

6 With medium-consistency red icing and a #3 tip, pipe a scarf between the head and shoulders of your reindeer.

7 Immediately pipe some skinny white lines on top of the red scarf with medium-consistency white icing and a #2 tip. Do not use a #3 tip. The white lines will spread and drown out the pretty red part of the scarf.

8 Pipe two . . . wait for it . . . egg shapes in the middle of the head for the eyes. Pipe them right next to each other and let them run together. Immediately add two beady little black dots with medium-consistency black icing for the pupils.

9 Use the same medium-consistency black icing to add a big ol' black nose. Pipe a drop of white icing on top of the nose and use a toothpick or scriber to pull it out into a shine line.

10 Repeat steps 6 and 7 to add the end of the scarf. Let it dry for an hour.

11 With thick white icing and a #1 tip, add a fringe to the end of the scarf. Use thick black icing and a #1 tip to add eyebrows and a mouth to your reindeer.

Ring

1 Use an ornament cutter and cut off the very top of the shape before baking according to recipe directions.

2 This step is optional. Outline and fill the cookie with white icing. You can use thick icing to outline and thin icing to fill it in. Or you can outline and fill the entire cookie with medium-consistency icing. It's your choice. Let it dry overnight.

3 Trace a small circle cutter with a yellow food color marker.

4 With thick gold icing and a #3 tip, pipe over the top of the circle you just drew. Try letting off the pressure on the piping bag just before you complete the circle to avoid a large end blob.

5 With medium-consistency gray icing and a #2 tip, pipe an upside down triangle at the top of the ring. Let it sit until the surface is dry—about 15 minutes.

6 Add a trapezoid to the top of the triangle. (You had no idea you were going to get a geometry lesson here, did you? Don't underestimate me. I'm full of surprises.)

7 Add details with a #1 tip and thick white icing and thick gray icing.

Ring Toy

1 Round off the bottom of some party hat cutouts. You can use a knife or a moon cutter. Bake according to recipe directions.

2 Pipe a half circle with medium-consistency taupe icing and a #3 tip. Let it dry for 15 minutes.

3 With medium-consistency pink icing and a #3 tip, add a rounded rectangle above the half circle. Let it dry for 15 minutes.

4 Continue adding different colored rounded rectangles until you reach the top. Let each layer dry before adding another. Pipe a ball at the top of the toy.

Rosettes

Rosettes are a fantastic cookie to throw into any set. They are quick, easy, and dry at lightning speed. They also add a great texture to a platter of cookies. These cookies use thick icing. Add one to two tablespoons of corn syrup to each cup of thick icing to keep the icing from being brittle and hard when eaten.

1 Drop a large flower tip (such as 2D or 1M) into a piping bag without using a coupler. These tips are larger than normal and won't fit on your regular couplers. Fill the piping bag with thick icing. Start between the center of the cookie and the outside edge.

2 Pipe one small circle and as you come back to your starting point, move your tip toward the outside edge of the cookie.

3 Keep the tip close enough to the first circle so that both circles slightly overlap. Pull the tip up and stop applying pressure as you complete the final swirl. That's it! I told you it was quick and easy!

Royal Icing Transfers

Sometimes the easiest way to re-create a shape or design perfectly is to trace the image. Royal icing transfers are icing that has been piped over a design and then allowed to dry before using. They are great for basic shapes and eyes. And while they can be incredibly useful for monograms or other intricate designs, they are also quite fragile. Dry royal icing doesn't bend. It breaks. Make sure that the design you choose doesn't have overly thin areas that will be weak once dry. A good way to make sure your transfers will be stable is to use a #3 tip to pipe them. Lines thinner than a #3 tip are easily broken. Pipe at your own risk. When you first start piping royal icing transfers, make at least 25 percent more transfers than you will need in case some break while transferring them to the cookie.

1 Draw or print the image you want to re-create. Tape it to a solid surface. I like to use the back of a baking sheet, but you can also use a cutting board or a book as well. Tape a piece of waxed paper or parchment paper on top of the image.

2 Use medium-consistency icing to trace over the top of the image. For very thin designs, considering allowing the first layer to dry and then piping over the top again. Let the images dry for at least 4 hours or overnight.

3 When images are completely dry, gently cut the tape holding the wax or parchment paper to the solid surface. Use a piece of paper to move the whole set of transfers to a flat surface that has a hard edge.

4 Very carefully and slowly pull the waxed paper over the hard edge. Pull the paper down across the edge so it pulls away from the royal icing images.

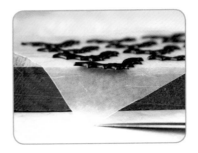

5 Use a thin knife to support the image as the waxed paper is removed. The knife can also be used to gently loosen the image if the waxed paper is sticking to it. Be very careful that you do not use the knife to lift the image up and away from the paper or you will break your transfer. And that will make you sad because you just spent hours and hours of your life waiting for these precious treasures to be ready.

Royal icing transfers can be placed directly onto wet icing. You can also "glue" the transfer to your cookie by placing a small amount of royal icing on the back of the transfer before gently pressing it onto the cookie.

Royal Icing with Meringue Powder

Ingredients:

⅓ cup meringue powder

⅔ cup warm water

7½ cups powdered sugar (2 pounds)

1 Tbsp. vanilla extract

Place meringue powder and water in the bowl of a standing mixer. Grab the whisk attachment and swirl them around together for a few seconds. Attach the whisk and mix on high for 3 minutes. It should be frothy. Scrape the sides with a rubber scraper. Add powdered sugar and mix on high for 2 minutes. Don't turn it to high all at once or you're just going to get powdered sugar everywhere. Add the vanilla (or other flavoring of your choice) and mix on medium for about 30 seconds. Transfer to an airtight container. Use immediately or store covered in the fridge for up to 2 weeks.

• •

Royal Icing with Powdered Egg Whites

Ingredients:

¼ cup dried egg whites

¾ cup room temperature water

1 Tbsp. lemon juice

7½ cups powdered sugar (2 pounds)

1 Tbsp. vanilla extract

Mix egg whites and water in the bottom of a mixing bowl. Let it stand for 3–5 minutes. Add lemon juice, and beat on high speed until stiff peaks form. Add powdered sugar, and mix on medium just until combined. Add the vanilla extract, and mix for another 30 seconds. The resulting icing should also be about stiff-peak thick. I usually wait until after I color my icing before I thin it down. But . . . you know . . . do what you want.

NOTE: The lemon juice is for your protection. It will stabilize the egg whites. If you beat egg whites too much, their protein structure will be compromised, and they will sink and get all weird and then you will have to get rid of them. And probably cry. And then try all over again. But if you add lemon juice, they will beat at stiff peak phase for a while longer, giving you time to realize they are ready even though you totally got distracted by the fire truck that drove into the river across the street.

Ruffle Pumpkin

1 Use a pumpkin cutter to cut out cookies, and then bake them according to recipe directions.

2 I used a #97 tip for the ruffles, but you could also use a #103 or #104 tip as well. Keep the flat part of the tip close to the cookie. Keep the tip vertical as you move it back and forth.

3 Use extra-thick orange icing so the ruffles won't melt into each other. Remember, you can add corn syrup to the icing before adding the extra powdered sugar so the dried icing won't be hard to bite into. This is also a great cookie to make with butter cream icing. Pipe a small bundle of ruffles in the middle of the cookie.

4 Continue piping bunches of ruffles around the center, rotating the cookie as necessary for a random appearance in the ruffles.

5 Fill the entire pumpkin with ruffles. Use a toothpick to remove icing that went over the edges, if necessary.

6 Add a stem with medium-consistency green icing and a #3 tip. When making green icing for pumpkins, I always add some of the orange icing to the green so that the two colors coordinate better.

Sand Castle

1 Use a sand castle cutter to cut out cookies, and then bake them according to recipe directions.

2 Use medium-consistency tan icing and a #3 tip to pipe several towers on the sides of the cookie. Immediately add windows with medium-consistency brown icing and a #1.5 tip. Let it dry for 30 minutes.

3 Use the same tan and brown icing to pipe a wider wall and window in the center of the cookie and to add a roof to the tower on the left. Let it dry for 30 minutes.

4 Add a castle gate with the tan icing.

5 Use the medium-consistency brown icing and a #1.5 tip to add the parapets.

Sanding Sugar

Larger than regular granulated sugar, sanding sugar is very shiny. It is available in two different grain sizes—sanding and crystal. Sanding sugar is about twice the size of granulated sugar and crystal sugar is about ten times the size of granulated sugar. Sanding sugars can be used to create texture, dimension, and emphasis, and to cover mistakes. It comes in almost any color you can imagine, if you can find it. You can also purchase white sanding sugar and create your own custom colors. Place the white sugar in a ziplock plastic bag along with two to three drops of food coloring. Shake and massage the bag until all the sugar is a uniform color. Spread on a baking sheet in a thin layer to dry. Crystal sugar can lose its high gloss shine when recolored.

To apply sanding sugar to wet icing, place the cookie on a cooling rack over a paper towel and use a spoon to sprinkle sugar over the top of the icing. Allow the icing to set for three to five minutes before gently moving the cookie to a tray to dry completely. The paper towel can be folded in half and used as a funnel to pour the excess sugar back into its original container. Cookies with a thick layer of sanding sugar can take an extra two to four hours to dry. When the cookies are fully dry, use a culinary paintbrush to remove loose sanding sugar before storing or packaging.

You can also apply sanding sugar to dry icing. Mix two parts corn syrup with one part water and brush it onto the areas where you want the sanding sugar to stick. Sprinkle sugar on to the cookie as directed above and allow to dry for an hour before brushing off excess sugar.

. . . .

Saturated Colors

Colors like black, red, navy, purple, and pink can be tricky to mix without the icing tasting bitter. They require more food coloring than other lighter colors. It helps to remember that these colors will darken for a few hours after they are first mixed. Mixing these colors the day before you need them will help you use less food coloring than necessary. Another trick I love to use is adding my favorite flavoring to thin the color-saturated icing instead of water. The extra flavor masks the bitter taste of the food coloring and makes the icing taste amazing!

Scriber

This sharp pointed tool was originally used for markings in metal or woodworking. The food-safe version is called by the same name. You can either free-hand designs or etch around a template onto a cookie before starting. The sharp end is also very useful in guiding icing, popping bubbles, and drawing through the icing when creating wet-on-wet designs. I like the solid feeling of a scriber in my hands, but a toothpick will work just as well most of the time.

Sea Horse

1 Use a flip-flop cutter to cut out cookies, and then bake them according to recipe directions.

2 With medium-consistency blue icing and a #3 tip, pipe a head and body for the sea horse. I find it easiest to pipe the snout last. Let dry for 15 minutes.

3 Use a medium-consistency light-blue icing and a #3 tip to add fins, a coronet on the head, and 3 small dots on the stomach of the sea horse.

4 Add a large dot of medium-consistency white icing to the head with a #3 tip. Immediately pipe a smaller dot of black on top. Add a tiny dot of white with a toothpick where the two colors meet.

Spreading Cookies

Sometimes when young cookies get warm in the oven, they start pushing their boundaries and trying to figure out who they really are and they end up coming out looking not at all like the sweet little shapes you put in. Finding a solution other than grounding them until they reach cookie adulthood can be tricky. If spreading cookies is a common occurrence at your house, try these tips to help.

Start by using a recipe that is known for not spreading. None of the cookie recipes in this book spread. If you have an heirloom recipe that you can't bear to part with even though it has spreading issues, try dipping the cutter in flour before making each cut. Chilling the cutouts on the baking sheet for fifteen minutes before baking will also reduce spread. Also, giving those cutouts their space is imperative. If you overcrowd your baking sheet, the cookies will spread. Every time. Even with the "fantastic" recipes from this book I keep telling you about.

When the cookies come out of the oven, after all the love and attention you've given them, if they have still managed to spread themselves out of shape, you can quickly re-cut with the original cutter. Press down gently, but firmly and give the cutter just a little wiggle to help cut smooth edges.

Starfish

1 Use a starfish cutter to cut out cookies, and then bake them according to recipe directions. A traditional star cutter would also work if you bend the edges slightly before baking.

2 Outline and fill the cookie with medium-consistency yellow icing and a #3 tip. Let it dry for at least 30 minutes.

3 With medium-consistency dark-yellow icing and a #3 tip, pipe 5 large dots in the center of the cookie, corresponding to each ray. Pipe slightly smaller dots along each ray.

4 Immediately pipe smaller dots of medium-consistency light-yellow icing on top of each of the dots from step 3.

Stencil Genie

A stencil genie is an innovative tool designed to give you the extra three hands you need while using a stencil. The plastic square frame holds stencils in place over a cookie through the use of magnets. It comes in different widths to accommodate cookies of all thicknesses.

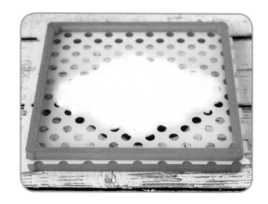

Stencils

Stencils are a great way to quickly add texture, designs, or backgrounds to a cookie or set of cookies. Stencils can be used with an airbrush, with icing, or by dabbing color onto the cookie through the stencil.

1. When using icing with a stencil, be sure to use a thick icing for crisp lines. I like to put my cookie on a metal surface and hold the stencil in place with craft magnets.

2. Use an offset spatula or bench scraper to spread the icing across the surface of the stencil. Spread the icing on the widest part of the design first. It will help keep the cookie from shifting under the stencil.

3 Smooth out the surface of the icing with the spatula before removing the magnets and lifting the stencil straight up off the cookie.

4 Use a toothpick to clean up any icing overhang on the edges.

5 Using stencils with an airbrush is a simple process. Try to make sure that you are spraying down onto the stencil and cookie as much as possible. If your airbrush is too low and sprays at an angle, you will get color under the stencil. This is known as "under spray" and will create shadows in your design. Some people find it beneficial to prop their cookie and stencil up at a slight angle to enable them to spray the stencil straight on.

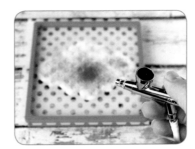

Storing Cookies

Once your cookie icing has completely dried (usually twelve to twenty-four hours), you need to find a place to store your cookies. They keep fresh longest when stored in an airtight container. This could be a sealed bag or in a rigid plastic container. If the cookies took a little longer than you anticipated while decorating and the cookies themselves have started drying out, you can revive them with a terra cotta disc. Sold as a "brown sugar saver," these discs can be soaked in water and then placed in a corner of your sealed container to give that moisture back to the air. Your cookies will absorb the small amount of moisture and freshen up again. This also works with a slice of bread. Make sure to place the bread or terra cotta disc on a piece of waxed paper and do not allow either of them to touch your cookies.

Sugar Pearls

Just like they sound, sugar pearls are shiny little round balls of sugar and cornstarch. They come in sizes from two to twelve millimeters and all colors of the rainbow. They can be used as flower centers, eyeballs, animal noses, decorations for Christmas tree cookies, confetti, and a jillion other things. They are hard like jawbreakers, but usually just taste like a giant sprinkle. You can recolor sugar pearls with an airbrush. You can also place them in a small lidded container with a drop or two of food coloring. Shake the container until the color is uniform and then spread them on waxed paper to dry. Be aware though—recoloring can make them lose their high-gloss shine.

Sugarveil

Sugarveil is a flexible icing made from a mix that allows you to bend and mold after setting. It is most often used with mats and molds to make lace or other types of fabric decorations, but it can also be piped. It can easily be colored by adding food coloring while mixing. Excess mixed Sugarveil can be stored in an airtight container in the refrigerator for up to five days. Once completely dry, Sugarveil can be fragile. Cookies containing Sugarveil should not be placed in an airtight container. The humidity can soften the Sugarveil and cause it to droop.

. . . .

Supplies

As the cookie decorating trend takes off, so does the availability of cookie decorating supplies. Cutters, bags, tips, cookie molds, and Sugarveil lace mats—you can find the tools and supplies to decorate almost everywhere you look! You no longer have to rely on special ordering from an outdated catalog. Grocery stores have cookie cutters and kitchen stores have aisles full of piping tips and food coloring. The following is a list of great places to look, but don't let it limit you. The best finds are always in the most surprising places.

Brick and Mortar Stores	
Hobby Lobby	Sur La Table
Jo-Ann Fabric and Craft	Walmart
Michael's	Williams Sonoma

Online Shopping	
www.artfullydesignedcreations.com	stencils and gifts
www.brpboxshop.com	cookie and bakery boxes
www.thecookiecountess.com	stencils and airbrush colors
www.cookiecuttercompany.com	tin cookie cutters and basic baking and decorating supplies
www.coppergifts.com	custom and standard copper cutters and basic decorating supplies
www.creativecookier.com	cookie cutters, stencil genie, and basic decorating supplies
www.giftsintl-us.com	packaging materials

Online Shopping (continued)	
www.globalsugarart.com	cookie and cake decorating supplies
www.karenscookies.net	cookie cutters and basic decorating supplies
www.nashvillewraps.com	packaging materials

Toy Soldier

1 Use a thin rectangle cutter to cut out cookies, and then bake them according to recipe directions.

2 Pipe a rounded square shape with medium-consistency dark-blue icing and a #3 tip. Let it dry for an hour.

3 Use medium-consistency skin-colored icing to pipe a rounded face.

4 Pipe a tall rectangle in the center of the cookie with medium-consistency red icing and a #3 tip. Pipe two thinner rectangles on either side for arms. Allow to dry for 30 minutes.

5 Add shoulder epaulettes, a belt buckle, and hat details with medium-consistency yellow icing and a #2 tip.

6 Use thick white icing and a #1.5 tip to add uniform details. Use skin-colored icing to pipe dots for hands.

7 With thick black icing and a #2 tip, add eyes and a belt.

Tuxedo

1 Use a gift cutter to cut out cookies, and then bake them according to recipe directions.

2 With medium-consistency yellow icing and a #2 tip, pipe a small bunched square shape at the top of the cookie. Let it dry for 5 minutes.

3 With the same icing, add the bows to either side of the bow tie.

4 Use medium-consistency gray icing and a #2 tip to pipe the collar. Imagine piping a heart to help you get the right shape.

5 Fill inside the collar with medium-consistency white icing and a #3 tip. Outline and fill below the collar with medium-consistency light-gray icing and a #2 tip. Let it dry for 30 minutes.

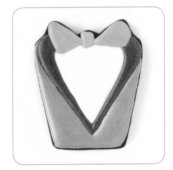

6 Outline the bow tie with thick yellow icing and a #1.5 tip. Use the gray icing and #2 tip to pipe a pocket on the bottom right side of the tuxedo.

7 Use thick white icing and a #1.5 tip to pipe two parallel vertical lines for the shirt. Add buttons with the gray icing and a #2 tip. Finish the cookie by piping a triangle-shaped handkerchief in the pocket with yellow icing.

Valentine's Day (See *Double Heart, Flowers in a Jar,* and *Kissing Lips*)

Vanilla Sugar Cookies

A chewy variation on the classic sugar cookie, these cookies are soft and won't spread.

Ingredients:

1 cup slightly softened butter

1 cup brown sugar

½ cup granulated white sugar

2 extra large eggs

2 tsp. vanilla

¾ tsp. salt

¼ tsp. baking powder

4–4½ cups flour

Cream the butter and both sugars together. If you have any brown sugar lumps, you should crush them up or pull them out. They make weird dents in your baked cookies. Add the eggs and the vanilla, and mix thoroughly. Add the salt and baking powder, and again mix the dough.

Before you add the flour, let's have a little chat. Different altitudes need different amounts of flour. Differences in humidity will the change the amount of flour you should add. Is there a storm coming? That changes things. Add only 3 cups to begin with. Then add additional flour ½ cup at a time until the dough is no longer sticky and holds together. (This happens at about 4 cups of flour for me . . . except in the winter time when it happens at 3½ cups flour.) That's when you should stop if you are going to chill the dough, or just wait for another day to bake it. If you are going to roll it out right away, add another ½ cup of flour so it will be thick enough to move from rolling out surface to your baking sheet.

Bake at 350 degrees. If you roll to ¼-inch thick, bake for about 7 minutes. If you roll to ⅜-inch thick, bake for about 10 minutes. If you want crunchier cookies, bake them until the edges are just turning golden brown.

. . . .

Vintage

One of my very favorite things to do to a cookie is to make it look old and dirty. I don't know why. It really doesn't seem like a good idea. Sometimes I just can't help it. I like things that are worn. It's like you can trust them, you know? Not that you really need to be trusting a cookie . . . but just in case, here is how you do it.

1 Your cookie needs to be completely, absolutely, without a doubt dry before you start to make it look vintage. Grab a food-grade paintbrush, some water, and a paper towel. Place some drops of brown, green, and black food color on a paint palette or plate.

2 Dip your brush in the water and gently blot the excess water onto a paper towel. Use the damp brush to pick up a mix of the food coloring.

3 Paint it on the edges and in the crevices of your cookie. Work in small sections.

4 Dip your brush in the water again, but don't rinse it. Use the watered down food color still in the brush to "wash" the rest of the cookie. You need to work quickly or the surface of the icing will start to pit and look like a sponge. And unless you're making sea creatures, that is not what we want.

5 Quickly and gently wipe the excess water and food coloring off the cookie. Repeat on any remaining sections of the cookie.

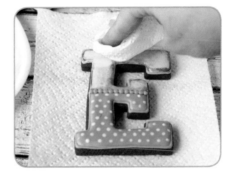

6 You will be left with a beautifully aged cookie masterpiece that you can totally trust.

Wedding (See *Cake*, *Flowers in a Jar*, and *Tuxedo*)

Wet-on-Wet

This is a term that describes any design where one color of icing is placed on top of another color of icing before the bottom icing has had time to dry. Advanced preparation of all colors is necessary as icing usually starts to crust over within minutes. This technique is especially useful for polka dots or stripes, or any design that requires a flat surface with multiple colors.

Wood Grain

1 Use brown icing to pipe your background for the wood grain. Let it dry overnight or for at least 8 hours. While your icing is drying, place 4–5 drops of white food coloring on a small plate along with one drop of chocolate brown and one drop of black food coloring. Let these dry overnight as well.

2 Dip a flat brush in some water and gently pat on a paper towel. The brush should be wet, but not dripping water. Brush across the white food coloring with the entire brush. Brush across the brown food coloring with just the tip of one edge of the brush and brush across the black food coloring with the tip of the other side of the brush. If you were to paint a vertical line right now, you should be painting stripes of brown, white, and black.

3 Paint across the cookie horizontally. Reload your paintbrush as necessary, taking care to keep the brown and black on the same sides of the brush. Overlap each stroke and occasionally go back and paint over harsh lines. Everything looks strange and wrong when you first start, but as you continue to blend the colors, it will create a seamless depth of texture.

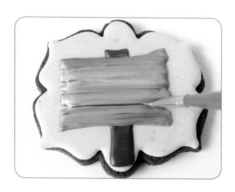

4 Turn your brush on the brown edge and paint thin lines to mark the edges of the boards.

5 Use the very thin tip of the brush to paint small detail grain lines. Allow to dry completely before piping on top of the wood grain if you desire.

Z

Zebra

1 Use a bell cutter to cut out cookies, and then bake them according to recipe directions. If necessary, cut the top handle off the bell before baking.

2 Turn the bell upside down. With medium-consistency pink icing and a #3 tip, outline and fill what is now the bottom portion of the cookie. Let dry for 30 minutes.

3 Outline and fill the remainder of the face with medium-consistency white icing and a #3 tip.

4 Use the white icing to outline the ears. Immediately fill with the pink icing.

5 With medium-consistency black icing and a #2 tip, pipe stripes on the side of the face and give this guy a mop of hair on top of his head. (If you are concerned about color bleed, use dark-gray icing instead of black. No one will notice. I mean, I used dark gray. Did you notice?)

6 Use thick black icing and a #1.5 tip to pipe eyes, nostrils, and a mouth. You can give your zebra some pink cheeks with luster dust or food coloring.

INDEX

ABOUT THE AUTHOR

GEORGANNE BELL is the sugar artist behind the popular cookie decorating blog *LilaLoa*. Georganne was an instructor at the international Cookie Convention in 2014 and 2015. She has had her cookie projects published in *Cake Masters* and *American Cake Decorating Magazine*. She is a regular contributor at SugarEd Productions Sugar Art School and was a guest instructor at Kyeongpuk Culinary College in South Korea. Georganne has been on a local morning television show as well as McGoo U, an Internet cookie decorating show. She also gives plenty of unsolicited advice and occasionally does laundry before it becomes strictly necessary. You can visit her at www.lilaloa.com where she will tell you everything you ever wanted to know about decorating cookies.

0 26575 16959 1